Choose a Better Life

Common Sense for Uncommon Living

By Stephanie Hester

Choose a Better Life: Common Sense for Uncommon Living

Choose a Better Life
2300 Declaration Drive
Raleigh, NC 27615

ISBN: 978-0-9728638-1-0

The author may be contacted at the following address.

Stephanie Hester
Choose a Better Life: Common Sense for Uncommon Living
CABLBook@gmail.com

CREDITS
Editorial assistance by Jessie Hyer
Cover designed by Elissa James at www.elissajames.synthasite.com
Photography by Chuck Hester
Additional assistance by Chris Morrissette and Jack Tackett

First Printing: July 2009
Printed in the United States of America

10 9 8 7 6 5 4 3 2 1

To my husband Chuck who is a great travel companion on this journey of life. Thank you Honey for being so willing to grow with me.

And for my daughters who continue to challenge and teach me. You all hold a special place in my heart that can never be filled by anyone else.

I love you.

Contents

Welcome to Choose a Better Life

Call it self-fulfilling prophecy or the power of suggestion. Whatever you call it, we, as spiritual beings, have been created with significant authority over our lives. We have been given the opportunity to decide whether we will grumpily survive life or live a life of passion and joy. Personally, I choose the latter.

Our lives are made up of a series of choices. Once we realize this we can take control of those choices and Choose a Better Life. When we deliberately make choices with intention we can focus on the positive, generate energy and passion, and open the door for a better future.

Sound idealistic? Perhaps. But realistic? **Definitely!**

Regardless of your spiritual beliefs, we have the amazing opportunity to shape our futures. But how we shape them is completely our choice. And whether we realize it or not, we make these choices every day. Moment by moment we choose our response to what happens around, and to, us. We can opt for grumpiness or we can choose happiness and joy.

I hope you will join me in *Choosing a Better Life*.

How to Use This Book

Choose a Better Life: Common Sense for Uncommon Living is divided into seven sections, Personal Development, Passion, Relationships and Forgiveness, Words, Health, God-Sightings, and Hodgepodge. Each section is comprised of several mini-chapters or as I like to call them, tidbits of treasure. Each tidbit of treasure is designed to be a quick read, providing a specific tip for Choosing a Better Life.

Each of these tidbits is taken directly from a personal life lesson. Because of this, you may notice what at first appear to be contradictions. These are not contradictions, rather lessons I have learned to varying degrees and some with which I still struggle. As with anything worth doing well, Choosing a Better Life takes effort and practice.

It is my hope that as you read through this book you will not rush. Instead, as you read each tidbit of treasure take a moment to think through ways it can apply to your own life. Then, become aware of your choices, intentional about your actions, and determined to Choose a Better Life.

Personal Development

- 1 -

Introduction

Personal development is one of my favorite topics. Maybe it is because I realize there is still so much I have to learn or maybe it is simply because I feel good after I have integrated something new into my life. I love to challenge myself ... to try new things or to learn a better way to accomplish something I'm already doing.

I even love to overcome my fears. I am, for example, afraid of heights. But I climbed the Sydney Harbor Bridge, 456 feet above the water, with my husband when we were in Australia a short time ago. It was a wonderful and exhilarating experience. I was proud of myself for attempting it and was rewarded with amazing views of Sydney.

Personal development is about so much more than just reading a book, although that is a great place to start. It's about embracing the lessons this world has to offer and integrating them into your own life. It's about challenging yourself to grow and learn, enriching your experiences and increasing your quality of life.

Personal development is a gift we give to ourselves and for each one of us it may look differently. I may need to grow in the area of discipline whereas you may have mastered that trait. You may need to grow in the area of patience whereas your spouse has more patience than he needs.

But one thing is for certain. Our personal development is personal. No one can give it to us and no one can learn our lessons. It is up to each one of us to individually take control of our lives and choose to learn from our journeys. It is only then that we can grow and mature: part of Choosing a Better Life.

- 2 -

Musings from a Broken Vessel

I often wonder how I can feel able to take on the world at one moment and feel like a heap of broken earthen-ware the next. I can walk into a room of the who's who in the business world and commandeer the floor, but two hours later sit alone in my office and not be able to pick up the phone to return a call.

My only conclusion ... I am broken. In my humanness and in my selfishness I do not always function at my optimum. (That is not to say that I am not effective or efficient, I can be obsessively so, or that I am not "put together," people are often mislead because I appear to be extremely self-sufficient.)

But it does mean that I desperately need to retreat, be introspective and acknowledge my brokenness. I need to be honest with myself, acknowledge my weaknesses and recognize that I do not have it all together and I most definitely do not have all the answers. It is only by doing so that I can give all my pieces to God knowing that He is the ultimate Craftsman.

In a way that only he can, God takes my broken pieces and molds them into something beautiful and useful. And in His hands I can be anything. I can be the friend who brings encouragement, or the mother who says the right words when her daughter needs them most. I can be the acquaintance who shelters a family from harm or the stranger whose willingness to be vulnerable in a blog changes someone's life. In His hands I can even be the hero a desperate student so eagerly awaits. And yes, I can be the businesswoman who impacts a community.

So, it is sitting in my brokenness that I am most thankful. For it is only then that I realize apart from God I can do nothing, but in him I can do all things.

We are all broken. But it isn't until we acknowledge our brokenness that we can allow the One who created the universe – the farthest star my eye can see as well as the puppy that sits at my feet – to use us in ways far greater than all we ask or imagine.

Choose a Better Life by embracing your brokenness, giving all the pieces to God, and letting Him mold you into the best you you can be.

- 3 -

Make a Difference

My husband and I live a "Pay it Forward" lifestyle. We firmly believe that we have been placed on this Earth to, among other things, bless others. So we look for ways – some small, some large – to help.

Unfortunately, many of us feel as if we are too small to make a positive impact. "I am just one person, what can I do?" Honestly, one person can change the world. Mother Teresa and Martin Luther King Jr. are just two examples, albeit well-known examples, of this fact.

"But I am not Mother Teresa, I don't have her compassion. And I certainly don't have Martin Luther King, Jr.'s charisma." Maybe not, but you do have your unique gifts and talents... gifts and talents that, with some creativity can be put to use to make a difference in your environment.

Along those lines, I read a blog post that illustrates how little it would actually take for us to make an everlasting impact on this world and some of its "bigger problems." This post stated that if just 4% of the world's population donated just $1 a week we would have a NET of $ 11,094,720,000.00 [Just over 11 BILLION DOLLARS] every year at our disposal.

That $11 billion could be used to provide health care for the poorest families. It could be used to end world hunger. It could provide quality education for the millions of children who never set foot in a school. It could provide safe housing for the world's homeless. The possibilities are exciting and endless.

However, you don't have to tackle the world's biggest issues to make an impact. You can begin by simply meeting the need of a neighbor. One of our friends was given a gift certificate from his employer as a Christmas gift. The gift certificate was for a men's clothing store that specializes in suits. Because our friend doesn't wear suits to work, he passed the gift certificate along to someone who was looking for work. This act of "paying it forward" cost our friend nothing, but meant a great deal to the recipient.

Choose a Better Life by challenging yourself to come up with unique ways to impact the world around you.

-4-

Noble Character

I often think about my character. How do I act when no one is watching? Is my public image the same as my private one?

Character is defined by the Encarta Dictionary as "the set of qualities that make somebody or something distinctive, especially somebody's qualities of mind and feeling."

Often people try to project a specific character or persona when they are in public. They want to be recognized for specific traits and behaviors. Inevitably, however, no matter how focused we are on our public image, it is our core character that people eventually see... it is our core character that comes shining through, especially in times of stress or anxiety. Because of this, I don't want to create a false image that I have to try to maintain.

It is important to me that the persona I project when holding a workshop or consulting is founded on truth and is the same one I have when I'm doing the laundry. Granted, I am much more energetic and animated in my workshops than I am in my laundry room, but my core beliefs, values and attitudes are not different. I truly believe in the value of "what you see is what you get." I don't have anything to hide and I don't pretend to be something other than who I am.

When our kids were little we used to tell them that telling the truth frees up their minds because they don't have to try to remember what they said. Conversely, when they told a lie, they would have to remember exactly what they said so their following statements would support the lie. Eventually this becomes a jumbled mess of tall tales that they could not keep track of and the truth inevitably came out.

This same principle applies to our persona. It is so much easier to tell the truth, to be authentic, to be real about who we are from the onset.

When I was growing up and I'd complain about a challenge my father would smirk and say, "It builds character." I didn't quite understand what he meant, but there was a great deal of truth in what he said.

Lately, one of my specific prayers has been that I would be a person of noble character. I want to act with purpose not react to situations in life.

One of the best ways to develop our character is to embrace the challenges life throws our way. Instead of running from them, grab a hold and pull them in close. Struggle with them and learn from them. Let the challenge grow and strengthen you.

Choose a Better Life by choosing to develop your character and be real about it with others.

- 5 -

Reframing Failure

All too often we tend to hold on to failures and forget successes. As a career change instructor I saw this in my clients. CFO's to on-air personalities to office assistants, most of them share the same things: fear of change and lack of confidence in their abilities. It is the later on which I want to focus.

I often asked my clients what job/career path, resources unlimited, they would like to pursue. What employment opportunity would give them the most satisfaction? Most clients were quick to identify a career they'd like to try. But when I asked why they were not pursuing that path I was met with a host of excuses ... everything from, "I'd never be able to do that" to "I just don't have the right training."

Not having the correct training is definitely a valid obstacle. However, it is not an insurmountable one. There are numerous ways to get training: college courses, specialized schools, night classes, on-the-job training, volunteer opportunities, etc. Not having the training just means you will have to add that component to your plan of action.

The biggest barrier to pursuing dreams is the "I'd never be able to do that" belief. When I pushed my clients a bit further on this statement inevitably their responses came back to lack of confidence. And the lack of confidence most often stemmed from a previous failure; a failure that may not even be remotely related to the opportunity in question.

Why is it that we so often hold on to our failures with a death grip? Is it because we've been told we would fail and now we are afraid to try again? Is it because we want to protect ourselves from future failures? Is it that a wounded ego won't let us let go? Or is it simply because we don't know how to let go of failure?

Whatever the reason, when we hold on to past failures with determination, we are selling ourselves short and compromising our quality of life. We are choosing to stop believing in ourselves which leads to our being comfortable in our misery and unwilling to take risks.

Instead we need to practice reframing. We must redefine failure not as a sign of weakness but rather as another opportunity to learn and grow. At the minimum, a non-success teaches us what doesn't work. And anytime we gain insight and wisdom we are making progress.

Read about men and women who have overcome the odds, who have not let failures stop them from pursuing their dreams. Add some of these people to your mentor category and let their stories encourage you to look at your failures as stepping stones to your future successes.

Don't be afraid to have faith in your abilities and in the person God made you to be. Step out and pursue your dreams. You will make mistakes along the way. Good. Learn from them, grow your knowledge base and continue moving forward.

Choose a Better Life by choosing to reframe your failures as learning experiences and opportunities to refine your goals.

- 6 -

Starting Fresh

Often when we set a goal for ourselves we do so with gusto, expecting nothing to stand in our way of achieving it. But as we pursue that goal sometimes we run into unexpected obstacles that we allow to stop us in our tracks. Other times the monotony of daily living just simply wears us down and we let go of the goal we had wanted to achieve.

Very few of us pursue our goals with the fervent passion required to reach them without looking back or getting distracted. Most of us start with good intentions, but lose steam when the stresses of life (a sick child, a less-than-supportive spouse, a micromanaging boss, financial concerns, etc) pressure us.

Instead of getting discouraged, I challenge you to start fresh. Just because you've stopped working towards a goal does not mean the goal no longer exists. Somewhere inside you the desire that moved you to set the goal originally is still there. You just need to regroup, revisit the passion and begin again. The only thing that is stopping you is you.

The pressures of life will always exist. None of us are exempt from them. But each of us has a choice to how we respond to them. You have the power to choose whether or not these pressures derail you from pursuing your goal or make you more determined to reach it.

This choice is one I had to make recently. Because I was so very ill a few years ago I value good health like never before. But in order for me to remain healthy certain things must be a priority for me. I must eat well, avoiding gluten, dairy and sugar. I must exercise regularly. And I must get enough sleep. Easy enough, right? Wrong.

Several months ago I began letting some of my routines slip. First, I stopped taking my supplements three times a day. Then I let time pressures squeeze out my exercise routine. A few months later I began sampling foods that I knew were not good for me. Before I knew it some of my symptoms were returning.

The more the symptoms returned the worse I felt and the less motivated I was to make a change. And in the middle of this was when I came down with micro pneumonia.

I had a choice to make. I could continue to feel bad and let my circumstances (fatigue, arthritis-like pain, all-over achyness, foggy thinking, etc.) dictate my quality of life or I could decide to start fresh... to go back to my original health plan where I would have to start over.

I chose to start over and I am so thankful I did. As with everything, this is a process. It will take time for me to get back into full swing of a completely healthy lifestyle, but I am already seeing improvements in the way my body functions.

Are you like me? Do you have a goal for which you need to start over? Have you let the pressures of life thwart your momentum?

Choose a Better Life by choosing to start fresh. There is no reason why you shouldn't.

- 7 -

Live in the Moment

If you are a parent I'm sure you've said something along these lines to your kids, "Don't be in such a hurry to grow up. You only get to be a kid once." I've said this to my daughters on many occasions. My youngest one seems especially eager to get to certain milestones in her life – dating, going to high school, driving, etc. I guess that partially comes with being the last of three daughters to "grow up."

But what is interesting, is that I could be saying the same thing to myself. No, I don't want to be older, but I often find myself looking ahead and looking forward to what is to come. In and of itself, this is not a bad thing, I'm a huge proponent of being excited about the future, but when we let the future rob us of the present we are doing ourselves a disservice.

How many times have you said to yourself, "Wow, this month has gone by fast" or "I can't believe Spring is already here?" Or, looked at your child and wondered, "Where did the time go?"

On the flip side, how often have you found yourself in the middle of one activity thinking about what you will do next? Or, if you're like me, you've driven to a destination just to realize you don't remember the drive.

I'm an advocate of planning and goal setting, but all too often we move from one task to the next without enjoying the present. The adage "stop and smell the roses" holds a lot of truth.

We need to slow down, smell the roses and live in the moment, <u>this</u> moment. We need to stop wishing our lives away by looking so forward to, or worrying about, what is to come that we ignore what we've been given – the here and now. Once today is gone, we will never get it back again.

Choose a Better Life by choosing to live in the moment and enjoying the present. Life is full of wonderful moments if we would just stop and experience them.

- 8 -

Laughter

I've read that children laugh 300 to 400 times a day. Adults, however, laugh on average only 15 times a day. Why is that? I'm sure it can be argued that adults are under more pressure and stress than kids. (Although, spend a day with any teenager and you will find that they are under a great deal of pressure and stress too.)

I wonder at what age we begin to stop laughing. Is it in middle school when peer pressure starts to intensify? Is it in high school when we begin to feel the weight of the world on our shoulders? Do we stop laughing in college when the pressures of career choices become reality? Or does it just simply happen over time?

I don't know the answer to those questions, but I think the more important question is: Why don't we laugh more now? Aside from the health benefits of laughter – it reduces stress, increases endorphins, burns calories, etc. – laughter is just plain fun.

In my home we laugh and giggle a lot. We enjoy jokes, laugh when we play with our dogs, laugh when we play board games, tell stories and laugh with friends. As a family we eat dinner together most days and laugh at each meal. We work hard at building laughter into our lives.

I love watching tears seep out of my husband's eyes when he is laughing so hard he can't talk. My daughter ... she's a snorter. She tries to control her laugh, but when she is really cracking-up she begins to snort, which only makes her laugh harder.

As for me, I've got a unique laugh. I've been compared to windshield wipers, a hyena, and numerous other things. When I laugh in public I get quite an array of responses. Sometimes people look away as if they don't want to "catch" what is going on, sometimes they move to other tables, but mostly they can't help themselves and they end up laughing too. (I have actually had a waiter put a paper bag over my head in hopes it would help calm me down – I have a picture to prove it.)

But as unique as my laugh is, I wasn't aware of it until after I went to college. I don't remember laughing much as a kid and I don't ever recall seeing my parents laugh. Laughter was just not valued in my family's household and it was not a part of my growing up years. Maybe that is why I love it so much as an adult ... I am making up for years of not having heard my own laugh.

Whatever the reason, I love to laugh and I love to hear other people laugh. Laughter eases hurts, relieves tension and sets the stage for a great day. Ultimately, laughter is a small way of spreading cheer.

Choose a Better Life by choosing to laugh. Laugh with others, laugh by yourself and laugh at yourself. Life is much too short to live it grumpy.

Blessing Road Rage

I read an article in a magazine published by my insurance company. The article stated that although the most extreme form of road rage, when we use our vehicles as weapons, only occurs 1200 times/year, there are over 400 billions other incidents of aggressive exchanges on the road each year. 400 billion! That number is astonishing. These aggressive exchanges include things like driving close to someone's bumper in an effort to get him to change lanes or slowing down and deliberately not changing lanes when someone is riding your bumper.

I have a better idea. When you feel someone has done something to "wrong" you on the road, instead of fighting back or yelling or honking your horn, say a simple blessing over him. I started doing this several months ago and I've noticed that the time I spend in the car is much more enjoyable. The traffic isn't any better and I still come across people who cut me off or drive 20 MPH in a 45 MPH zone, but it no longer stresses me out or angers me.

Instead of my knee-jerk reaction to call the offender names or slam on my horn or complain about the drivers in my city, I've trained myself to simply say a blessing over the other driver. Usually my blessing is short, "I bless you in the blue Mazda today. I bless your family, you job and your finances." That's it. I'm done and ready to move on.

One of the things that is so great about blessing is that instead of my getting agitated - my jaw locked, my muscles tense, my attitude bad – I smile and simply go about my business having avoided all the negativity that would have affected the rest of my day.

In addition to the personal benefits, blessing others is fun. It's the ultimate gift in paying-it-forward. By blessing the other driver I have opened the door for good things to happen to him, things that he isn't expecting and things that will hopefully surprise him. And hopefully these things will positively impact other people he comes in contact with throughout the rest of his day.

Learning to bless someone who has angered you is a process. I didn't start by blessing the other driver's day, family and finances right away. I started with fun and funny things that enabled me to defuse my anger first. I'd bless the other driver's cat, dog and/or hamster. Then I'd bless things like his home and yard. It didn't matter whether or not the driver actually had pets or a home, the point was to get me to a place where I could actually bless him and mean it.

This is a tactic I still use. So much in fact, that the joke among some of my friends and family has become, "Watch out, if someone is blessing your dog you know you've done something to really tick him off!"

Regardless of where the blessing starts, by simply opening your mouth and offering a blessing instead of a curse you are impacting the other person, your own attitude and the world around you in a positive way.

Choose a Better Life by preempting your anger and offering a blessing to those who would otherwise frustrate you.

- 10 -

Looking Forward

Many people take the first few weeks of January to set New Year's Resolutions. I've never been a big fan of resolutions, but I am a proponent of goals and priorities – whether they are set at the beginning of the year or throughout. That being said, regardless of today's date, take a few moments to reflect on the previous year and plan for the coming one.

A few thoughts to help you get started:

Celebrate the good. As you look back on the last 12 months remember all the good things that happened throughout the year and celebrate them. Even for those of us who had struggles to overcome, there are always God-sightings, places where we can find joy in the midst of the darkness – a smile from a loved one, a word of encouragement from a friend, a step taken toward achieving a goal, a new business relationship, etc. Think back to those times, be thankful for them and celebrate.

Prioritize your time. We are always presented with more opportunities than we have time to take advantage of. It's when we try to do them all that we run into trouble – we become over-stretched, overburdened and overwhelmed. This year, commit to doing less, better. Pick the few things that align with your priorities and do them well. Say "No" to the rest.

To help pick you priorities answer this question, "If you could only achieve one thing in the next 12 months what would it be?"

Schedule time for yourself – every quarter. I schedule personal retreats … time away with just myself, God, my Bible, my journal, my laptop and a great book. I am not able to able to take such an extensive time each quarter, but I understand the vital role time to myself plays in my mental sanity and as such scheduling this time is a MUST. You need to do the same. Schedule time for yourself.

Schedule time for your friends and family. With all the craziness in our lives we often take our friends and family for granted. Unfortunately, it is not until we move away or lose a loved one that we realize how much we miss them. Make sacrifices where necessary to ensure you have time with those you love. Your quality of life will improve with every minute.

Renew old acquaintances. Is there a friend you've lost touch with? A mentor who impacted your life? An old co-worker you learned from? Find five people you want to get in touch with and contact them. Tell them of their importance in your life and thank them for taking the time to make an impact.

Pay it forward. Look for ways you can bless someone else without expecting anything in return. When asked how you can be repaid, simply say, "Pay it forward." As you bless others you will receive joy by watching the ripple effect of blessing pour forward.

Most of all, expect great things! Remember, your actions are dictated by your beliefs. So if you believe great things are coming your way you will act accordingly and open the door for abundance.

Choose a Better Life by reflecting, learning from, and celebrating the past as you plan for the future and expect great things.

Passion

Introduction

Passion is defined by Wikipedia as an intense emotion compelling feeling, enthusiasm or desire for anything.

Passion helps give our lives meaning. It motivates us and carries us through when the next step seems too difficult to take. When we are living passionately, pursuing the things that stir our emotions, life is so much more enjoyable.

Many people associate following our passion with work, what we do for a living. But a passionate life is so much more than that. It is how we live: embracing life, defining experiences, and spurring us on to greater things.

One of our blessings is living in a world that offers us infinite choices about which to be passionate. Just as no two people are identical; neither should the things that drive us be identical. I may be compelled by relationships or humanitarian causes. You may be enthusiastic about making people laugh or finding homes for abused animals. The options are as endless as the number of people on this planet.

Part of Choosing a Better Life is defining your passion, embracing it, and allowing it to propel you into action. May the tidbits of treasure in this section help you do just that.

- 12 -

Pursuing with Passion

My daughter's favorite movie star was in the next town filming a movie. A few weeks prior my husband and I decided I would take the day off and take her to where we thought he was filming for the day. We were thrilled to discover we had the right location.

We, along with several other fans and a television news crew, waited for hours in hopes of catching a glimpse of this man. Imagine the excitement when he actually took a few minutes away from the set to come out and great everyone. He chatted with the girls and signed autographs.

Most of the fans, my daughter included, were so star struck that they could barely talk, but they sure did giggle quite a bit. Once the movie star went back inside the buzz among the fans continued. "Oh my gosh! I can't believe I met him!" "He is so amazing."

We had started the day just hoping to see this start, but we had come prepared with movie paraphernalia in case the amazing happened ... an actual meeting. And it did.

What I found intriguing was that after the star returned to the indoor set and his PR rep said he would not be coming back outside the girls wanted to stay. I tried to explain to my daughter that she had gotten more than she initially hoped for and that this star would not be coming back outside until after the end of shooting – 10:30 pm – and I was not willing to stay that long.

In the days that followed my daughter continued to talk about her encounter. I thought about my daughter's passion (ok, almost obsession) with this movie star and her willingness to endure endless hours in the sun just to see a glimpse of him again. Her desire to have a connection with this guy propelled her to put aside everything else just so she could focus on him.

I began to wonder what I pursue with that same fervency. What do I pursue with that same non-stop passion? What possibilities get me so excited that I am willing to set everything else aside just to get a glimpse of something great?

Imagine how wonderful our world would be if we took the same burning passion my daughter has for this star and used it within ourselves to propel us towards our goals. What would our businesses look like? What about our neighborhoods? What if we dedicated ourselves to making a difference in this world? To impacting the lives of those around us? The possibilities are endless.

Choose a Better Life by choosing to release your passions and pursue them with fervency. Don't let the grind of daily living get in your way. Pursue, pursue, pursue.

- 13 -

Mentors, Champions and Encouragers

One of my passions is to use my writing and speaking engagements to help others grow while encouraging them to make choices that lead to a better life. In doing so, I've met some fantastic people who support me in this journey.

My Mentors remind me that following my calling really is my only option. Anything else would be slighting God and limiting His work in my life.

My Champions are the ones who rally around and believe in me when I begin to doubt my decisions.

My Encouragers, some whom I've never met, are those that relate how my stories have impacted their lives.

I value and need each of these people more than I can say. I thrive on hearing how a word or thought I've shared has given someone strength or hope. I rely on my Champions to carry me when I'm frustrated with my progress. And I am thankful for the exhortation to stay the course that only my Mentors can provide.

That being said, not everyone is a believer in what I do. Many people think I should be working a "traditional" job that earns a steady income to help care for my family. Some of these folks have even gone so far as to tell me I won't "make it" in my chosen profession. Others have been much less blatant in their attempts to deflate my dream by simply pushing their negativity on me.

One of the lessons I quickly learned is that I need to rid myself of toxic people. Yes, toxic people. You know the type. Those that say, "You're going to do what? Are you sure that's what you want to do?" Or "That will never work. Give it up." These are the people who, rather than catching my vision, seem to push their own agenda.

Toxic people come in other forms too. They may not be attacking me directly, but they sure do zap my energy and make me feel bad when I am around them. These are the people who are always negative. They hate their job, never seem to get a break and are always having problems with someone. For these folks the weather is never right, the politicians are always wrong and the problems of the world are always on their mind.

Toxic people … get rid of them! Now I'm not necessarily advocating cutting off friendships with your lifelong pals, but I am saying that if you want to make things happen in your life you need to surround yourself with people who will help you reach your goals.

Find the Mentors, Champions and Encouragers. Focus on the relationships that bring you strength, happiness, and courage. Encircle yourself with those that challenge you to take the next step; those that will cheer for you from sidelines and run onto the field to give you a shoulder to lean on when you need it.

In the same way, be a Mentor, Champion and Encourager for others. Be the person people seek out and want to be around. Be the one who says, "Yes, you can do it. Keep going. Don't give up."

Choose a Better life by believing in you and believing in others. Find passionate people and enjoy the energy that will motivate you to live your dream.

- 14 -

Discover You Passion

So you've surrounded yourself with Mentors, Champions and Encouragers; you have reframed your view of failure; and you have decided to make a decision about your career – you want a change. What's next?

Discover your passion.

Passions are interesting things. They can move us emotionally, excite us about taking action and ignite a blaze in our souls that is inextinguishable. But many of us claim not to know what our passions are.

Hogwash! I argue that we know what our passions are, but we have spent so much time telling ourselves that we can do nothing about them we have squelched our ability to hear them. We have, in essence, buried them alive.

We must make it a priority to rediscover our passions and allow them to breathe new life into our daily lives.

Take a weekend away, or a day or even a few hours. Go someplace where the minutiae of daily life will not interfere. Ask yourself questions such as:

When do you feel the happiest?

What angers you the most?

What gets you the most excited?

As a child, what did you dream about doing?

In school, what activities did you enjoy?

If resources were unlimited, where would you go? What would you do?

What tasks do you enjoy doing most? Which ones do you like least?

If you could communicate one truth to the next generation what would it be?

When you die, how do you want to be remembered?

Give yourself permission to dream and feel again. Listen to your heart without filtering the responses.

We are each created in a unique way, with unique passions that should be driving us. And until we free these passions and allow them to move us, true fulfillment will not be ours.

Choose a Better Life by making the time now to rediscover what your passions are. Don't put it off until the timing is better. There will always be distractions in life, but you owe it to yourself – and those around you – to be the best person you can be.

- 15 -

After Passion Comes Action

I hope you have taken the time to identify your passions ... the things that get your heart pumping and get you excited about living. Assuming you have taken this step, now what? It's one thing to know your passions, and another to live them out.

Pick the two or three items from your Passions list that you are moved by the most. Write each on the top of a blank sheet of paper. Focusing on only one at a time, list all the ways you can become engaged in and incorporate this passion into your life.

For example, one of my passions is encouraging women through sharing "my story" and the blessings I've received through life's challenges. So my list of ways to get engaged included: blogging, writing articles and books, joining women-focused clubs/groups, speaking at women's events, etc.

As you brainstorm ways to get involved don't filter your thoughts. Let your imagination flow. Some ideas will be unrealistic, but many will be completely feasible. Once you've exhausted your own thinking, enlist a friend or two. They will have a different perspective and will add great value to your ideas.

Next, pick two or three possibilities from your new Ways to Get Engaged list and come up with doable action items, steps you can take to achieve each idea. My steps for getting articles published, for instance, included: taking a "How to get published" course, researching writing markets that are of interest to me, brainstorming potential article ideas and sending out queries. Your action items will be unique to you and your passions.

The important thing regarding your steps is that they are doable. Think of them as mini-goals. Goals are only valuable if they are obtainable. You very well may have to stretch yourself to achieve them, but they are definitely within your reach.

Finally, and most importantly, take action. If you are committed to living a vibrant life you must be willing to work to get there. Making lists are only helpful if you put action behind your words. Commit yourself to taking one step toward your passion each and every day. Your step doesn't have to be Earth-shaking. It may be that today you research companies who provide the service you are passionate about, tomorrow you may register for a class, the next day you may begin seeking a mentor, and so on. The vital thing is that you take action.

Living your passion takes a willingness to risk ... risk that comes with stepping out of your comfort zone. But with each step you take, the risk becomes less threatening and your goals more attainable.

Choose a Better Life by taking action and living your passions.

Taking Risks, Big Payoff

Everything we do in life comes with risk. Whether we are driving our children to school or reaching out to meet our neighbors or stepping into a new leadership role, everything we do comes with some measure of risk. So, why is it that we so often fear taking risks?

There are a few of us thrill-seekers who enjoy taking risks, at least in some area of our lives. But most people become fearful and anxious when they think of stepping out of their comfort zone and doing something different. Hearts begin to race, palms become sweaty and emotions well up. Taking risks scares us.

I believe it is because we buy into Webster's definition of risk. It says risk is the "exposure to the chance of injury or loss; danger." By that definition risk is negative.

But what Webster's doesn't include, and what we often forget, is that risk offers a tremendous payoff. The satisfaction and growth we can get out of taking a risk, whether or not we achieve "success," can be tremendous.

Take for example, the single mom who goes back to school to finish her degree so she can pursue a better career that offers more stability for herself and her family. Big risk. Big potential payoff.

Or my friend Paul who got his degree in accounting only to discover his passions lay elsewhere – in entertaining people. In 1999 he wrote and rehearsed a one-man variety arts show and founded Flow Circus to fulfill the mission of promoting life-long learning and play through the Variety Arts. He has been performing ever since and he loves it. Big risk. Big payoff.

Taking risks does not come without, well ... risk. On some level you must be willing to sacrifice one thing for another. And in most cases, the thing sacrificed is comfort. When our lives get into a routine we tend to get comfortable. Changing any part of it means we risk losing that comfort.

In my case, I have sacrificed a "regular" "stable" job to pursue my career of passion. As such, I find things along the way that I need to tweak and I sometimes stumble over mistakes. But by pursuing my passions and following what I am called to do I also discover that I am stronger and more capable than I thought. I am also constantly growing in new ways and experiencing joy like never before. This makes me a better wife, mom, friend and leader. And it provides me the opportunity to positively impact the lives of people I come in contact with – my ultimate goal.

Choose a Better Life by choosing to take a risk, even if that risk means trading your comfort for the unknown.

- 17 -

Become Child-like

My husband and I were having dinner with a few friends, who also happen to be business associates. As we were eating we were sharing ideas and stories.

One gentleman who owns his own business said that he dislikes talking to his father on the phone because no matter how well business is going his father always has something negative to say. He also said that whenever he shares his ideas for new business with his father, his father always focuses on the potential problems and declares, "That will never work."

Everyone around the table could relate. Not all of us have parents who shoot us down, but we all knew someone who was ready to squash our ideas and dreams the moment we shared our vision.

But what was interesting was that those of us who were parents ourselves (our kids ranged in age from 13-21) all agreed that when we share our ideas and dreams with our children not one of them shoots us down. Quite the contrary. Most of the time our kids are our biggest supporters and they often come up with additional ideas to incorporate into our vision. They tend to see the world as a place full of possibilities.

As my friends and I discussed this we agreed that as we grow into adulthood we tend to become jaded and less free-thinking. We filter information through our life's experiences and what we have witnessed in others.

Unfortunately, this filtering can make us negative. And it's this negativity that puts us into the "toxic people" category and diminishes our value to others. This same negativity also makes us less likely to take risks.

What we need to realize is that taking risks is what often leads to great successes. And if in taking a risk we fail, we need to embrace that failure as a learning and growth opportunity by which we refine our efforts for the next attempt.

We also need to encourage those around us when they take us into their confidence by sharing their visions and ideas. Unless we are specifically asked to do so, it is not our job to look for the potential setbacks or problems and deflate someone's dream. We are much more valuable when we cheer others on and root for their success.

Choose a Better Life by choosing to be child-like. View the world as a great experience waiting to happen. Be willing to view risk as positive and be supportive to others who do the same.

- 18 -

Passionate About People

I love people. I love that everyone has a story.
Everyone.

Some people's stories include a difficult childhood,
others a loving home life. Some lived overseas; others have
never left their hometown. Some people are intertwined with
sports, others are academics. Some were given the best of
everything; others had to drop out of school to help support
their families. The options are as endless as the number of
people.

But everyone I meet has a story. I wish I had time to
hear them all. I'd love to get to know the waiter who served my
family and me brunch and the man who stood behind me in line
at the post office. I would love to know more about the lady
who sits in the lobby with me at the doctor's office. She and her
husband are shy and don't like to talk much so I don't probe.

But whenever I have the chance, I ask questions and
listen to stories. And what amazing people I have met.
Ordinary people with extraordinary lives.

I met a former CIA agent in the bookstore. His wife is
German and he has 3 kids, 2 sons and 1 daughter. He has lived

all over the world and speaks several languages. We had a great chat not too long ago.

I met an Egyptian man who now lives in Sydney, Australia. He has a fantastic family and an amazing heart for his kids. He teaches classes at his church when they need someone to fill in. And he loves owning his own business so he can be available for such occasions.

I had the opportunity to forge a friendship with my neighbor. She is from the Middle East and is often left at home to take care of the kids while her husband travels back "home" to work. She and I moved to North Carolina about the same time and we helped one another study for the driver's test. Because she is Muslim and wears a hijab I had the opportunity to vouch for her when she took her picture at the DMV.

I was able to share parenting stories with the technician who did my last mammogram because we both have kids about the same age. My heart was saddened when she told me one of her children passed away early on. But I was inspired by how she was determined not to let that be the only thing that defines her.

I have literally met people from all over the world and been blessed by listening and sharing part of our lives. Even the folks I've chatted with in passing at airports have enriched my life as they widen my understanding of the world and the people in it.

I love to hear stories. Everyone has one and no two are alike. Even siblings who grew up in the same family have different experiences and interpretations of the events of their lives. The more stories I hear the more fascinated and encouraged I am by the fact that no matter where we are from, we all share commonalities including: love for others, the desire to be known and understood, and dreams for our future.

Choose a Better Life by taking the time to invest in the lives of others. Listen to their stores and if appropriate, share part of yours. People are wonderful and our lives are enriched by their presence.

- 19 -

Passionate About Priorities

I find it interesting that when life is the most hectic we tend to cut out the things that are the most beneficial to ourselves – time alone, time to exercise, quality time with our families, time out with friends. Unfortunately, these things tend to fall into the "not mandatory for survival" category.

Yes, it is true that we can survive life without the richness of time spent with friends or family. We can survive without exercise. And we can survive without time alone. But surviving isn't living. Living is what makes life enjoyable. It is what makes life fun and eventful. And living should be our goal.

I was reminded of this while I was in the process of re-branding my business – new company name, new logo, new website, new messaging, just about everything was new. Although this process was very exciting it was a lot of work, more than I expected honestly.

I had been feeling the pressure of not enough hours in my day.   As this pressure was building I had been forced to cut some things from my schedule. Unfortunately, I had cut the wrong things.

The first thing to go was my morning quiet time. This is time I take to pray, journal, bless those who are brought to mind and just rest in the "peace that surpasses all understanding."

The second thing I cut was some one-on-one time with my daughter. She was on summer break and she would have loved to spend days on end with me. Although I treasure my time with her and recognize it will not last forever, I had been saying "no" to time with her in lieu of "focused work time."

But interestingly, because I had cut two of the most precious things in my life, my "focused work time" had not been very focused. I struggled to get my thoughts together and was not nearly as productive as I needed to be. So, the pressure continued to build.

Finally, it dawned on me ... in order to be productive during the work-day I needed to nurture my personal life – my mind, my spirit and my soul.

So I decided that no matter how jammed my day was, I would start each and every day with my quiet time; time to get myself focused on the really important things in life. Then I decided that I would let my daughter pick one weekday, any day she wanted for just her and me to hang out. No calls. No email. No work.

And amazingly, but not surprisingly, the pressure began to release. I still had the impending deadline and I still had a lot of work to get done, but my mind was renewed. I was refreshed and refocused. I did not have more hours in my days, but my days were much more productive because I worked much more effectively.

This was a great reminder to be passionate about my priorities.

Choose a Better Life by remembering your priorities and making sure your schedule includes time to nurture yourself.

- 20 -

Who vs. Do

My husband and I had lunch with a woman from our area whom we met through an online social media site. Within a few minutes we knew there was an affinity for each other so when my husband had to get back to work, my new friend and I stayed for an hour or so longer getting to know each other.

Our conversation covered many topics including, family, work, vision, faith and authenticity. One of the things we shared in common is that when getting to know someone new, neither of us likes to focus on the person's job. "That is what they DO, it is not the WHO of who they are" she said. I couldn't agree more.

So often when we first meet someone regardless of whether it is a business function or a social event we ask, "So, what do you do?" We immediately delve into the person's job and how they make a living. This is understandable because many of us tie our self worth into our professions. But our professions are just a portion of who we are.

At the most basic of levels I am an author, speaker, and consultant. But I am also a wife, mother, daughter and sister. And more than that, I am a woman of faith who enjoys many hobbies, travel, and adventure. I have dreams and goals and love to try new things. I also have struggles and challenges. All this and more goes into the Who of who I am.

I think of lyrics from The Who's song "Who Are You." Part of the chorus says:

> *Well, who are you? (Who are you? Who, who, who, who?)*
> *I really wanna know (Who are you? Who, who, who, who?)*

All too often we spend such an enormous amount of time developing the Do in our lives that we forget about the Who. We have career goals and benchmarks that we agonize over and strive toward. In and of themselves career goals are not a bad thing. But when we allow that to be the focus of our lives, we miss out on so much more.

When I was in college my goal was to have a corner window office. I didn't care where that office was, I just wanted what it signified ... success. By the time I was in my mid-twenties I had that office. It was over 200 square feet and in a prime office park.

Like many others, what I soon realized was that the office, my Do, was not giving me the satisfaction I had desired. In fact, I was bored with my job and began looking for something else within a year or so.

But in the years that followed, as I began developing my Who, my Do was not nearly as significant and self-defining as it once was. Good thing. A few years later my husband and I lost our consulting business in a business deal that went bad and I lost my Do completely. I was unemployed. It was a challenging time, but I realized my Who and my character was what would remain with me.

And it is your Who and your character that will always remain with you long after your career has ended.

Choose a Better Life by being equally, if not more, passionate about developing your Who as you are your Do. And as you get to know new people focus on Who they are and share Who you are rather than your professions. Your relationships will be more authentic, rewarding, and sustainable as you dig deeper into each other's character.

Relationships and Forgiveness

- *21* -

Introduction

I heard someone say that happiness can be measured by the strengths of our relationships. I don't know that there is any empirical data to support this, but I do know that the state of our relationships has a direct impact on our quality of life. Few other things cause us mourn so deeply or rejoice so greatly as our relationships.

And one of the greatest hindrances to rewarding relationships is forgiveness, or should I say, the lack of forgiveness. All of us know the details of an event where we were wronged. Many of us even remember the locations, time of day, and the clothes the offender was wearing when this offense occurred.

Other than on the rare occasion we have grown from these experiences, what good do these memories do for us? None. Generally speaking, we use these memories to justify our anger, bitterness, and resentment. And as these negative emotions fester, they rob us of the job-filled life we could be living.

What I've learned about forgiveness is that it is an activity, not an event. Forgiving someone, for whatever it is they have done, isn't usually a one-time occurrence. It is something that needs to occur repeatedly as we delve through the layers of our pain.

Forgiveness is paramount in our relationships and in our ability to Choose a Better Life. It offers us the freedom we desire and opens our hearts to glorious relationships that nurture and bless our lives.

- 22 -

Being Open and Vulnerable

  I was having dinner with a dear girlfriend and although she doesn't struggle with her health as I do, she finds herself in a situation similar to mine. She has great excitement and anticipation for the future, but is having to wade through all the uncertainty of the present and wait for things to unfold. Exactly how things unfold will determine whether she and her family will be able to return home to Europe or have to stay in the States for an undetermined amount of time changing their professions to accommodate the move.

  But as she and I shared over dinner, I was struck by what a blessing it was to have each other. By being vulnerable with one another we could share our deepest burdens lessening the weight we felt we were carrying. At that point, our souls started to sing. By the time we had finished our salads we were crying from laughing so hard that people around us began to stare.

  At one point, through cackles and howls, my girlfriend said to me, "Really Stephanie, I'm not laughing at you ... it's just ... well, yes I guess I am laughing at you." All I could do was join her because the situation I was describing was so absurd there was no other way to deal with it. What an amazing salve to the soul laughter can be.

As we drove home I smiled and told my friend that I was glad she was stuck here in the States. I didn't have to explain myself and she didn't get defensive. My girlfriend knows I truly want her and her family to get back to their home as soon as possible. But she also knows I plan to take advantage of our time together as long as we have it. She would expect nothing less.

As I rejoice in our friendship I realize that I've really only known this lady for a few short years and most of that time she was living in Italy. But because we were willing to be open and vulnerable with each other from the start, our friendship has grown deeply and quickly and has become a great blessing to us both.

Choose a Better Life by choosing to be open and vulnerable with a friend. Yes, there is always a risk in sharing your heart, but the rewards that come back to you will far outweigh the risk of taking the first step.

- 23 -

Boundaries

I have discussed toxic people both on my blog and in this book. This has generated a question about toxic people who are close relatives. The specific question was "How do you get rid of a toxic person who is also a close relative?"

Getting "rid" of a toxic person, close relative or not, is harsh language. I am not advocating labeling people as toxic and then cutting off all ties with them. What I am advocating is that we realize all our lives are touched by toxic people in one way or another – the relative who has nothing but judgment to share, the co-worker who is always complaining, the neighbor who is always negative. The goal is to not let these people define us and drain us of our energy.

We need to find Mentors, Champions and Encouragers (see chapter 12) and surround ourselves with them. These positive people will be the ones who energize us and propel us on to greater things in our lives.

As for the toxic people, the best way to handle them is to set boundaries. Close relative or otherwise, it is our job to protect ourselves from the damaging negativity toxic people spread. We need to believe in our value, respect ourselves and let others know we expect the same from them.

However, in setting boundaries we must treat the other person with love and respect too. Sometimes this can be done simply with a conversation. "Susie, the other day when we were talking I felt judged by your statement of [insert comment here.] I realize you may not agree with my stand on this issue, but it is my belief nonetheless. If you'd like to discuss it I am open to doing so, but only if that can be done without judgments."

Obviously, not everyone is going to respond to this type of statement. You may have to take a firmer stand and even cut a conversation short. It may be, as is the case with me, that you only share minimal conversations with "Susie". And there will be times when your boundaries are not well received. Unfortunately, those relationships may be ones that are naturally severed.

There is a great series of books on this topic by Dr. Henry Cloud and Dr. John Townsend called *Boundaries.* Although the principles in these books are Christian-based they apply to everyone.

I want to stress that while we are setting boundaries, it is imperative to have healthy, positive, encouraging relationships in our lives too. We need people who will cheer us on, encourage us to look at all angles of a project or problem and let us know we are making an impact on our world.

Finding these people may prove to be a challenge, but don't give up. Be proactive, look around you and see who is in your life. Regardless of the depth of your current relationship, if you find someone you think can be a Mentor, Champion or Encourager approach him and ask if he'd be willing to "join your team." Not only will he be flattered (who doesn't want to be acknowledged for what he has to offer?), but you may gain an invaluable relationship.

Choose a Better Life by choosing to set healthy boundaries and surround yourself with positive people.

- 24 -

Forgiveness with Boundaries

Of all the things I do to care for myself one of the most rewarding is a personal retreat. A few times each year I go away by myself – just my journal, pen and a book or two. I spend time alone with God to reflect, relax and plan. It is a wonderful few days and I recommend it to everyone.

During one of these retreats I came to the realization that I had suppressed some wounds that had been inflicted upon me years ago. I had not thought about these particular wounds in a long time, at least not in the light of examining them and the effects they still have on me. It was a very painful process, but one that I am most grateful for having gone through.

As I walked through and examined these wounds I realized that the only way for me to truly break free of them was to forgive the people who caused the wounds. But for the first time in my life I understood that forgiveness comes on two levels. There is my forgiveness of the offenders before God and then there is my forgiveness I give to the offenders when they ask for it.

The great news is that the first and most important level of forgiveness, forgiving the offender before God, is not dependant upon the second, forgiving the offender when he asks.

As long as I come before God with the desire to forgive the person who wounded me, He can apply his salve and heal my wounds. No longer is my healing dependant upon the offender's repentance, or even acknowledgement, of the hurt. I can be set free from the bondage and pain of sin committed against me just by bringing it to God!

Another reality that set in during my retreat is that forgiveness does not necessarily equal trust. My offering forgiveness to someone, whether before God or to the person, does not mean that I must automatically trust him. When he wounded me, he broke my trust.

This is a simple concept, but it's one that I didn't understand before. I thought that when I forgave someone I needed to be willing to enter back into relationship with him and "pick up where we left off." That is not the case. I can forgive someone and still set healthy boundaries with our relationship. In fact, it is my responsibility to myself to set those boundaries and protect my emotional and, when necessary, physical health.

For me, there is a tremendous amount of freedom in this truth. I am now able to receive healing through forgiveness for offenses that I was previously unwilling to let go of because I was using them as an excuse to put up walls. I am free from the bondage of pain and hurt. And I understand that with that freedom comes the ability to protect myself with healthy boundaries ... not walls, but boundaries. Boundaries that say: I am valuable, I am worthwhile, I am healthy and I am not willing to put myself in a situation where you can hurt me again.

(I need to say that setting healthy boundaries is different from putting up walls that isolate you from everyone. Healthy boundaries show respect for yourself and others while providing the opportunity to make deep connections with people who share that respect.)

Choose a Better Life by taking your hurts to God, offering forgiveness and allowing Him to apply salve to the wounds. It's only then that you will be set free from the bondage of pain. And how wonderful is that freedom!

- 25 -

Freedom Through Forgiveness

Now that I have acknowledged my wounds, taken them to God, forgiven the one who caused the wounds and allowed God to heal my hurts, what is the next step? Is there a next step?

In regards to my particular situation, the offender doesn't even know he has done anything wrong. So, I've wondered if the "right" thing to do is tell the offender what he has done and the pain that has resulted. Several times I've sat down to write a letter to this person. I've thought through exactly what I'd say and how I'd convey the pain I've lived with for so many years. But each time I start to write, I stop and question my motives.

If I've truly forgiven him (remember, that doesn't mean I am giving him my trust), then I am not out to seek revenge. I no longer want to hurt him just because he has hurt me. So, I have to ask myself, why am I writing him? Honestly, my answer has always been the same, because I want him to acknowledge what he's done, repent and ask for forgiveness.

But the reality is that when I've broached similar subjects with this person, he has not acknowledged my pain.

Instead, he portrays the situation as meaningless and "water under the bridge." So, what do I do?

I toyed with this question for several weeks and it wasn't until I had lunch with a woman much wiser than I that discovered the answer. In relating similar wounds from her past my beautiful friend said that she has realized God's healing is enough. She understands that bringing up pains to her offender will not result in anything positive because her offender is not ready to, or capable of, dealing with the truth. And because of this, my friend would not get any resolution or closure that she does not already receive from God.

As my friend shared her story with me I realized that this applies to my situation as well. The person who wounded me is no more able to deal with the situation today than he was when he first committed the sin against me. So, there is no point in even trying to discuss it with him.

As I mulled this over and prayed about it I realized that I am okay with it. I don't want to lash out or seek revenge. I don't want to cause more pain or frustration. Instead I want to honor God with my actions. So I bask in the truth of who I am in Him – His daughter that He loves with a love that is far deeper than I can comprehend and His daughter that He sees as whole, complete and beautiful – and trust His healing touch to be more than sufficient to heal even my deepest wounds.

And if/when God sees fit for the conversation to be had with the person who wounded me, I will trust Him to guide my words and give me wisdom in the moments when I need it most. And if that time never comes it is of no consequence, because in Him I Choose a Better Life through the freedom of forgiveness.

Do you have wounds for which you need to do the same?

Choose a Better Life by choosing to take them to God so you can experience the incredible freedom that only he can give … the freedom that comes in spite of other people.

- 26 -

Expectations

Having planned several women's retreats, I'm always excited when I get to attend one just as a guest. Once such opportunity arose and all I had to do was share part of my story on the final morning. How wonderful it was not to have to coordinate any of the details.

After getting settled the first evening, I was disappointed to find there was virtually no structure to the night's activities. In fact, there was little apparent structure the entire weekend. Some things were given a timeline. Meals, for example, had to be eaten at specific times. But overall, the activities seemed to be quite loosy-goosy.

About half way through the retreat I realized I was getting increasingly frustrated because my expectations of a structured retreat were not being met. This frustration was hindering my enjoyment of the weekend. So, I took some time to adjust my attitude and decided to look for the good things that could come from spending time with these women.

I am so thankful I did. I ended up sitting and chatting with a woman for several hours. I was able to hear her story and her heart's desires. It was a precious time with a new friend.

   This event reminded me that when we enter a situation with expectations we are, in essence, saying I have needs (real or perceived) and you (or the situation) need to meet them. If/when those needs are not met our tendency is to become indignant and put up walls. Those walls block us from any good thing that may be happening around, or to, us.

   We carry expectations with us when we attend events, go on vacations, travel for business, attend meetings, make presentations, buy new items, etc. Without our even being aware of them, expectations follow us everywhere.

   One area expectations seem to be the strongest, and tend to do the most damage is in our relationships. Whatever the relationship – spouse, friend, family member, co-worker – we desire, and often think, the other person should meet our needs. And oftentimes we believe the other person should know our needs/desires without our even telling him. When those needs/desires are not met, we get angry or frustrated, put up walls and many times shut down. What a recipe for disaster!

   It's a conscious decision to release our expectations and allow ourselves to be open to the unexpected.

   Choose a Better Life by choosing to become aware of your expectations and willfully letting them go. By doing so, you will enjoy life more and be blessed in ways you did not anticipate.

- 27 -

The Gift of Sacrifice

Good Friday represents a day of great sacrifice. That is the day my Savior set aside His desires and took on the pain and anguish that was meant for me so that I could have a better life, both here on Earth and for eternity. Although we may never appreciate the magnitude of Jesus' sacrifice, regardless of our faith, I think we can understand that a great sacrifice was made.

So, as I've been pondering that thought I've begun to wonder what sacrifices I've made for the people I love and value. When have I put aside my desires for the benefit of someone else?

How often have I really sacrificed something of great value to me? I have yet to give my wardrobe to someone in need. Yes, I have given bags of clothing to the local homeless shelter, but if I'm honest, the clothes I give away are not my "best" clothes or the ones I like the most.

I have never sold my home and given the profits to a homeless family. I have not turned my job over to someone who is unemployed. And I have never given someone free access to my bank account so they could buy food and supplies.

Thankfully, most of us will never be called to make "big" sacrifices like those above or be asked lay down our lives for a loved one, but we have the opportunity to sacrifice ourselves nearly every day.

When I choose to run an errand for a friend instead of finishing the project I'm working on, I give my friend the sacrifice of my time. When I choose to have my daughter's room painted instead of investing in a piece of furniture for myself I give her a sacrifice of my desires. When I choose to give a friend a gift of money instead of going to the movies I am offering her a sacrifice of my finances.

Thankfully, I have the ability to offer these "do-able" sacrifices to the people I love, and sometimes, to people I don't even know. And although these sacrifices pale in comparison to the One that was given for me, I am glad I have the opportunity to give, to show other people how special they are.

Choose a Better Life by choosing to sacrifice something of value for someone you treasure. It's a tangible way to give the gift of love.

- 28 -

Mending Fences

Our lives and emotions are like onions, you peel a layer off and there is another one underneath. We are wonderfully complex and multidimensional allowing us to enjoy experiences on many different levels.

But because we have so many layers, an issue we thought was resolved can show itself again when we least expected it. This happened to me.

I had worked for a long time on personal healing and had forgiven those who wronged me. After my forgiveness had been given I enjoyed many months of peace in regards to these individuals. Then suddenly I realized I was angry with these people again – very angry.

It took me several days of journaling, praying and talking with my husband to realize that I was not angry for the past, I truly had been healed and given my forgiveness, but angry because of how I felt I was being treated now. What was even more frustrating is that the people with whom I was angry are people that I so long to have a good, healthy relationship with.

As I was working through this I had several epiphanies. First, I realized that the hurt I feel over what "could have been" is probably shared by these people too. Secondly, I realized that they are probably clueless about the pain that they continue to cause and if confronted, they would say that was not their intent at all. Finally, I realized that they probably have no idea how I feel.

I have been hesitant about sharing my desire for a rebuilt, healthy relationship because of fear of rejection and additional hurt. However, I am fairly positive these folks feel the same way. Even though I am unaware, I can be fairly certain that I have acted in ways to cause pain and hurt in this situation as well.

So, I decided to take a risk. I've written a letter to one of these individuals telling him how I desire to have a relationship with him. I have not gone into detail about my hurt or about the others involved. I am focusing strictly on my relationship with him. I am hopeful that we can slowly begin to mend fences and start anew on our relationship.

I must say, once I thought about how each of these others must be feeling my anger dissipated almost immediately and I began to see them in a new way. Now I am excited to see what God will do in our relationships.

Choose a Better Life by being willing to look at a situation from another's point of view and being willing to mend fences.

Playing Together

I am a member of the Business Alliance at my daughter's middle school. As an alliance it is our pleasure to help narrow the gap between the business community and the students. One of the activities we provide is an annual Career Day in which we bring in people representing a variety of careers.

This year we were blessed with 53 speakers representing 53 different careers: everything from Crime Scene Investigators, to Reporters, to Mechanics to Fashion Designers.

At the last minute I was asked to fill in for a speaker who was not able to attend the event due to a family emergency. Happily I agreed to talk with two groups of 6th graders about what I do. To keep it simple, I told them I was a Corporate Trainer who is paid to play games.

Since I was dong this off-the-cuff I did not have any materials or props so I decided to have the students play some of the games I use in my workshops. Although I expected a little bit of resistance, I was taken aback by the number of students who were afraid to drop their guard and have fun.

I realized that middle school is about the time people start putting up walls. By age 11 we are very aware of cliques so we try to shore-up our hearts to protect ourselves from rejection.

The more I thought about this the more I realized that for most people, those middle school walls never come down. We often move into adulthood with the same fears of rejection and so instead of tearing down our walls we make them even stronger.

Before long we are living in our own fortress determined not to let anyone get to close or see the "real me." As a direct result, we often miss out on some of life's greatest opportunities to have fun because we are afraid of what people might think.

I am a huge proponent of games, not only in my workshops, but in life. In my workshops I use fun, silly games as a way to get everyone on the same page … to give people the opportunity to realize that regardless of title, we are all the same. … to begin breaking down the walls so they will be open to one another.

In our home, we use games the same way. We have family night where we turn off the TV and just spend time together playing games. My husband collects Monopolies so we are often playing one version or another. What we've found is that whether we are playing just as a family or have included friends we always have a great time. We smile, laugh and talk about a number of things that would otherwise not come up.

We also play silly games in public. We monkey-walk to the car, play tag in the park, play in the Fall leaves and just generally have a good time.

By being willing to do something that can be seen as "silly" or "childish" we open the door for communication and bonding: two things that are crucial to our personal development.

Choose a Better Life by breaking down the barriers and just having fun whether you are at home with family and friends or out in public. Your life and your relationships will be enriched. And I guarantee the majority of people who look your way will not be judging you, but will be wishing they had enough courage to do what you are doing.

- 30 -

Stuffing

    I was having dinner with a few girlfriends. We were having a great time sharing about our Thanksgiving weekend with all of its fun and a few of the challenges that come along with extended families.

    One gal in particular made me smile. She and her husband are newlyweds. They have been married just over a year and are now at the point of discussing holiday expectations – whose family do we visit when, what foods do we prepare, do we invite close friends or just include family members, etc. In talking with her I was able to reminisce about these very conversations with my husband and all the gaffes we made along the way.

    As only women can do, our conversation encompassed a number of topics and somehow managed to come around to Thanksgiving leftovers. I shared that as I was packing up the leftovers from our Thanksgiving dinner I noticed we did not have nearly as much stuffing left as I had hoped. My family loves stuffing and we only treat ourselves to it twice a year. In fact, stuffing is one of the most coveted Thanksgiving menu items we eat during the day.

What I noticed is that my daughter and I were both eyeing the leftovers, hoping we got to them first. When it was down to the last portion tension started to rise – Which one of us was going to get the last helping? I know this sounds incredibly silly, maybe it's because we are not "supposed" to be eating stuffing in the first place, but we started to get territorial. "You've had two small helpings, I've only had one." "Yes, but Dad hasn't had any" and so on.

As I was regaling my friends with the stupidity of this situation, it dawned on me … how many times do I let inconsequential things take up time in my life? How often do I ruminate over minor situations and waste precious time and energy on things that aren't of any significant consequence? All too often I'm afraid.

There is a great small book by Richard Carlson titled, _Don't Sweat the Small Stuff: and It's All Small Stuff._ How much better off we'd all be if we truly followed that principle, especially during the holidays. Life is too precious to let the small things cause friction and blemishes in our relationships.

Choose a Better Life by choosing to let go of the small things and give the stuffing to someone else.

Words

- 31 -

Introduction

As children we are taught the saying, "Sticks and stones may break my bones, but words will never hurt me." What a lie! We all know the deep pain that words can cause. Not one of us would willingly endure the piercing blow of verbal abuse.

But hopefully we also know the great comfort that comes with a verbal hug aptly spoken. Hopefully, we've experienced the warmth that comes with a friends' email or letter that says, "I understand. I'll be here for you."

Words can mend heartache, "I'm so sorry I hurt you. I never meant for that to happen. I'll do my best not to let it happen again" or tear someone down, "I can't believe you did that. What a stupid mistake,"

They can bless, "I am so thankful you are my daughter. You are such a special young lady" or they can curse, "You are an idiot. You'll never amount to anything."

As Pearl Strachan Hurd says, "Handle them carefully, for words have more power than atom bombs."

It is so easy to fall prey to sloppy verbal choices, but we need to be aware of the great impact our words have on other people. Part of Choosing a Better Life is choosing positive words. Using our mouths to build people up, not tear them down. Speak with intention. Choose to bless and encourage the people in your life instead of cursing and discouraging them.

- 32 -

Words are Like Toothpaste

My husband, Chuck, loves to use the illustration that words are like a tube of toothpaste; once they are out of your mouth, you can't put them back.

We all know what this feels like. You're having a conversation with a friend and *slip*, out comes something you did not intend to share. Oops. More often than not, a similar thing takes place in arguments. In the heat of the battle, as you are trying to defend yourself and take back ground, you say something hurtful. You drudge up past mistakes or hurl a spiteful word at your opponent. You are, after all, trying to "win" the argument, are you not?

But there in lies the rub. What does winning the argument really mean? Does it mean that you have coerced the other person to acquiesce to your view? Does it mean that you have slung enough arrows to break down your opponent so he surrenders? Or does it simply mean that the other person gives in out of tiredness or boredom with the conversation?

The majority of our conversations, I don't believe, are entered into with the hopes of ending up in a battle of the words and/or wills. However, since conversations occur between two or more unique individuals, inevitably we will come across subjects on which we disagree. What do we do at that point? Do we stuff our feelings and/or beliefs to keep the peace? By no means. But we can express ourselves without entering into a verbal war.

Chuck and I attend a marriage seminar hosted by our church every Wednesday night. After the teaching portion of the seminar we break into groups of about 12 and discuss the material. We are fortunate enough to lead one of these groups.

Throughout the last 6 months a recurring theme has been communication. Recently we were given a list of "Counseling Principles." These are tools that the marriage counselor often gives his clients in helping them strengthen their marriages. One of these principles stuck out to me and it was the topic of one of the group's discussions.

The Principle – "Pay attention to how your conflicts end and try that in the beginning." What he meant was that we need to be aware of our behavior when a conflict is ending and try to start the discussion with similar behavior.

For example, in our marriage we often end a conflict much quieter than when we started. The majority of the anger is gone from our voices and we are likely to be listening to what the other person has to say. It is only at this time that we can truly hear the other's hurt and respond appropriately.

So if we started our conflicts by listening and not defending ourselves or our point of view; by trying to understand instead of thinking about our next response; and by maintaining a normal tone and level of intensity in our voices we'd be much better off.

The same is true of any discussion. By keeping our cool and thinking of the end result we are able to avoid much of the hurt that often comes from disagreements. And as a direct result we are able to keep the proverbial toothpaste in the tube.

How much better life would be if we implemented this on a daily basis.

Choose a Better Life by becoming aware of your conversations, especially your disagreements, and paying attention to the words you use and the impact they have on others.

- 33 -

Three Simple Words

Yes, the three simple words the title refers to are "I love you."

These three words can turn a sour moment into something beautiful. They can diffuse anger, ease frustration, deliver smiles, warm hearts, bring comfort and give someone great joy. When used correctly, these three words are powerful.

I returned from a vacation where I was able to visit my old haunts and see friends and family. I am quick to admit that there is nothing like a warm embrace from a long-time friend followed by, "I love you" to make me feel missed. How I cherish my friendships.

While I was there, my daughter and I stayed with one of my closest friends (an old college roommate) and her family. What a blessing to be welcomed into their home.

My girlfriend has just had her second beautiful baby – her other child is a 5 year old gorgeous boy. As any new mother knows it is so easy to get caught up with the daily needs of a newborn and let everything else fade into the background. But

I noticed that my girlfriend makes a concerted effort not to let her newborn's needs overshadow her son's.

She is constantly saying to her son, "Hey little man, I love you." Even when the baby is fussy, crying, and demanding her attention, Mom never forgets to let her son know he too is cherished.

What stood out to me even more is that during times of discipline my girlfriend never loses sight of her love for her son. She would often say, "Honey, because I love you I can't let you do that. The answer is still no" or "Little man, I told you not to do that, but you did it anyway. I love you, but you need to sit in time out." Amazing.

I would be remiss if I didn't also point out that dad does the same thing. Almost every series of interactions is preceded with "I love you."

There is no doubt that these kids will know they are treasured. I am sure, as with every family, there will be times of testing and times when Mom and Dad's love is pushed to the limit, but I know these kids will be confident they have a safe place where they are cared for and loved … a place to which they can always return.

Three simple words can make such a great impact. I was honored to see my girlfriend's family in action. Love is the underlying current of everything they do.

Choose a Better Life by letting someone know you love them. Regardless of whether or not your love is reciprocated, truly giving it to someone will brighten your day and impact theirs.

- 34 -

Reaping the Rewards of Blessing

Although I don't completely understand how this works, I know that God has given us the opportunity and authority to speak powerfully over our lives. Because of this, I have trained myself to bless people and things that are important to me every day. Some days I am a little less focused than others, but I try to make blessing a natural part of my daily life.

One of the many areas I've reaped the rewards of blessing is in my finances. My husband and I had a successful consulting business several years back. Due to a joint venture that went bad, we lost everything – our business, our money, our home. As a direct result, we ended up with enormous debt in the form of back taxes and credit cards.

For several years there seemed to be no way out of the huge financial hole we were in. We were effectively unemployed for three years and once we did obtain employment we were living, like most people, paycheck to paycheck. There was nothing "extra" to save or put towards our debt.

A few years ago I decided to change my outlook on our finances. Instead of looking at our income as barely meeting our needs, I decided to bless our income and rejoice that our needs were being met. So, I began declaring blessing over our finances. Each day I verbally repeat something similar to this ...

> *I bless our finances. I bless our desire to get out of debt and our ability to do so. I bless our desire to be disciplined with our spending and our ability to make the best choices. I also bless our jobs that provide for our needs. I claim God's promise to do immeasurably more than I ask or imagine. I bless our ability to generate enough income to give to those around us who are in need and therefore, be a blessing in their lives.*

After I bless our finances, I go on to bless many other things, our relationships, our neighborhood, the specifics of our jobs, our daughters' relationships and their school days, our friends and their families ... anything that comes to mind.

And besides adjusting my attitude and setting the stage for a great day, I've seen amazing rewards come from those blessings. Relationships have been formed and strengthened, obstacles overcome and business deals come to fruition.

But one of the most tangible results has been in the area of our finances. We have paid off all our credit cards and our back taxes! Our money is stretched as we find amazing deals. A few examples, my youngest daughter found a beautiful dress for her formal ... for $3.99. Yes, three dollars and 99 cents. We have been given opportunities to attend movies for free and found a way to purchase fresh produce at a fraction of the regular cost. I am most thankful for these gifts.

To be clear, I am not saying that by speaking a few words your problems will disappear. However, when you embrace the authority you've been given to proclaim blessings you not only impact your attitude, but also your circumstances. And when we take this stand we can claim victory in our lives.

Choose a Better Life by choosing to speak powerful blessings over your life and those you care for. As a result you will be, need I say, blessed.

- 35 -

A Simple Thank You

On one of my husband's blogs he posted about saying "Thank you" and blessing others - a recurring theme in our lives. With his permission I share the following comment that was left on his site.

As a waitress, I have had to deal with a lot of grouchy "grumbling guys" that take their hunger pains out on me. If only every customer could read your post and learn to bless people for their services, doing what's right would be a lot easier... and everyone would be a lot happier and healthier. You're right; it all comes back to you in the end! Comment by Ashley — April 2, 2007

Ashley says it all. If we would practice blessing instead of cursing, everyone would be a lot happier and healthier.

Thank you Ashley for sharing and reminding us that every service we take advantage of, being waited on in a restaurant or otherwise, has a person behind it that needs to be appreciated.

Over a three day period our street was paved. I thought the crew was done and so I parked back in my driveway. A moment ago I heard a few of the paving crew return. I went outside to see if I needed to move my car. No, they were just cleaning up.

This gave me a great opportunity to bless. I thanked the guys for removing the little bits of asphalt that were left on sidewalks and driveways and went inside. And the great thing is, I really was thankful. I do appreciate not having to contend with the little pieces of tar left behind.

However, I could have taken the other approach and complained that the clean-up crew wasn't here yesterday and that I had to deal with asphalt bits all last evening. But what good would that have done? None. The debris would not have been removed any sooner and I would have left the exchange grumpy and would have made the clean-up crew grumpy.

You can imagine the ripple effect this would have. I grumpily walk through my day and snip at everyone I come in contact with, they then snip at the next person they see and on and on the grumpiness goes.

Instead, by simply sharing my appreciation with these men, I have, at the minimum, contributed to making the world a less grumpy place and at the maximum spurred these gentlemen on to blessing someone with whom they come in contact later that day. A ripple effect I'm proud to be a part of.

Choose a Better Life by looking, with intention, for someone you can bless today. No need to make it elaborate, a simple "thank you for [insert service]" will do. By doing so you will start a joy that may have a far reaching impact.

- 36 -

The Muddied Diamond

When my daughter, Britini, was in the 6th grade she came to me to vent about a bully at her school. This bully swears at the other girls, my daughter included, and threatens to punch them, among other things. I was trying to comfort Britini while getting her to look beyond her circumstances and see that the girl who is bullying is probably doing so out of pain and anger at her own life. And because of this pain and anger, I wanted Britini to not only let the mean words roll off her, but to also bless this hurting bully.

The idea of blessing your enemy is not an easy, or new, concept. People have struggled with it for years, me included. But what was really difficult for my precious daughter to understand was that God loved this other girl as much as he loved her. At that point in our conversation, Britini said, "But that's not fair! How can he love her when she is so mean as much as he loves me?"

Good question. "God loves her just as much as he loves you. But because she doesn't know him and because she is so mean, she doesn't get to experience his love and power like you do."

In discussing this with one of my girlfriends she put it this way, "There are three diamonds on a table. They are all of equal size cut and clarity. Because they are identical they each carry the same value. But one of those diamonds gets restless and jumps off the table (suspend your disbelief here) and into a mud puddle. You pick the diamond up and place it back on the table. The diamond is still a diamond. It still has the same value to you, but its beauty is covered by its actions – the jump into the mud puddle."

As my girlfriend and I elaborated on this analogy, we realized that people do the same thing in a lot of different ways. The bully is covering her beauty and value with the words she chooses and the pain she tries to inflict on others.

We do the same when we spew a curse on someone or eye them with the "if looks could kill" look. We also jump in the mud puddle every time we use our words to hurt someone else or when we distort/bend the truth. Our value is still the same, but our beauty and worth are hidden from the rest of the world.

It is those times that I am deeply grateful for repentance and forgiveness. I can approach the Throne of Grace and ask God to take out his cloth and clean me off. There may be consequences because of my actions, but He is always faithful to remove the mud and let me sparkle anew. He is faithful to do it every time.

Choose a Better Life by being aware of your words and asking God to wipe away the mud when you jump into the puddle.

Self-talk: Reprogramming the Mental Tapes

If you are like most people, you probably spend time cursing yourself without even realizing it. By cursing I don't mean pulling out alligators' tails and saying some sort of incantation, but what you do is cursing nonetheless.

How often have you said things like, "I am so fat?" Or "What an idiot. I can't believe how stupid I am." Or even, "I hate my life."

Every time words like these come out of your mouth you are opening the door for disaster. As spiritual beings we have been given authority over our lives and when we curse ourselves with negative self-talk we are actually giving the powers that be permission to fulfill our words.

In addition, the more we allow negative self-talk to come out of our mouths, the more we are programming our minds to think the same way. And negative minds beget negative actions. So negativity perpetuates more negativity.

The reverse is also true. If we love ourselves with our words we are programming our minds to love ourselves too. This, in turn, allows us to live a more positive life which enables us to approach others in this same light generating a more positive reaction from those around us. Positive energy perpetuating positive energy.

Training your mind and your mouth, however, can be a challenge. If you've allowed yourself to be inflicted by others' words or your own, most of us have, you have work to do. My husband helped me realize this several years ago. I had recorded mental tapes that played all the curses I, and others, had placed on myself. When I'd get frustrated I'd allow the old negative tapes to play and my words would reflect those messages.

Reprogramming takes work and diligence. Generally it does not happen overnight, but it is well worth the effort.

I made a list of several things I knew to be true of myself and wanted desperately to believe. Among other things, my list included: I am fearfully and wonderfully made (Psalms 139:14), I am worthy, my womanly body is beautiful, I am intelligent, I am a good friend, I am successful, etc.

I kept my list where I would see it and be reminded to repeat these things to myself on a regular basis. Sometimes I'd pick one or two of the items on my list and adopt them as my mantra for days or weeks at a time.

The more I read and verbally repeated my list the less power my old, negative tapes had and the more empowered I became. I began feeling restored, worthwhile and capable of facing what was to come.

This truth is one I wished I had understood earlier in my life. I spent years cursing myself and allowing the curses of others to take a hold of me. As a result, I have to continually work to break those curses and remove their power. However, the good news is that the more I do it the easier it becomes. And the number of negative tapes I have running through my head today are far less than they were years ago.

Many of us curse without even knowing it. We are, unfortunately, so used to hearing the negative that we don't even notice it.

Choose a Better Life by being attentive to your words. Listen to what you tell yourself. Change your negative self-talk into positive self-talk and begin reprogramming your mental tapes. As you do your life and self perception will be transformed.

- *38* -

Good Morning!

I am a proponent of conversations and strokes (those little "hellos" to strangers). I love surprising people with a smile and a hello.

This particular morning, after an awards ceremony at my daughter's school, I stopped by my favorite coffee shop. As usual, their staff was fantastic. By the time I got to the register three employees had greeted me and started small conversations. That is exactly why I love this shop ... they are friendly and make me feel appreciated.

After coffee I stopped to get gas. As I was at the pump thinking through my day I was pulled back into the present by a very warm, "Hello, how are you today?" The attendant was walking from car to car greeting each of the customers. The conversations weren't long, but he was attentive to each response and gave a reply back. I also noticed that when the customers asked him how he was, he did not give the same pat answer. Each time he used different words to express that he was well. And each time I watched a smile come across the customers' faces.

My husband and I were in New York City. While there, I had a fantastic time talking to everyone I met: business connections, store clerks, policemen, subway crewmembers, and random people on the streets. I was intrigued by how many people were surprised by my conversations. Cab drivers especially seemed to be taken aback that a fare would be interested in their stories. But each time there seemed to be an excited tone in their voices as we chatted.

People like to be noticed and feel connected. We like to be appreciated. And something as simple as a good-morning greeting can make that happen.

Choose a Better Life by taking the time to smile and say hello to those around you. Your simple words can make a difference in someone's day.

- 39 -

Engaging in Battle

Two people I care about had come under verbal attack in two unrelated situations. In both instances the attacks were fairly brutal as my friends' reputations and character were called into question. And although I believe we need to be willing to examine our character, these particular attacks were neither productive nor warranted.

As I listened to both people walk through their respective situations I could relate well to their desires to defend themselves and deflect the attacks. The easy thing to do would have been to return the verbal attacks engaging in, in essence, a battle. Our desire to be justified and accepted spurs us into thinking that if we prove the other person wrong we will be viewed as "right."

Unfortunately, engaging in this type of battle does nothing for our cause. Instead it relegates us to a place of resentment and anger and rarely leads to the result we were hoping for – vindication.

Instead of throwing daggers back and forth it is much wiser to disengage the attacker. When we refuse to participate in a verbal war we reduce the influence of the attacks simply by not giving them credence. We also remove ourselves from the pettiness that so often accompanies this type of exchange.

Choosing not to defend oneself against unwarranted attacks is difficult at best. But by doing so, we are elevated above the attacks often leaving the attacker to deal with his own discontent and repercussions.

Choose a Better Life by choosing to let verbal attacks go by the wayside. They are neither worth your time and energy to defend nor the stress of counteracting them. Choose to take the higher ground by not engaging in the battle.

- 40 -

Why Wait?

I wonder how many of us wait for a special event to tell the ones we love how we feel. I know for many people speaking words of love is difficult. But expressing words of endearment is something with which we must become comfortable … for the sake of those we hold dear.

I have worked to make love sentiments an intentional part of my day. My husband and I not only say, "I love you" often, but we end each email, phone call and IM with the same statement. I make sure I tell my daughter that love her each morning as I drop her off at school and every night before she goes to bed – and many times in between.

I've learned that "I love you" is not just for family. I often tell my friends how much they mean to me and I've become comfortable with saying, "I love you" as we part ways and send emails. (This was something I had to work towards.)

Why is it so important to me that my family and friends know I love them? I'm not entirely sure. It may be because as a child I rarely remember hearing those words spoken. Or maybe it is a result of watching friends lose someone suddenly and suffering with thoughts of, "If only I had told them." Maybe it is simply because I know how great it feels when I hear those words from someone I hold dear to my heart.

Whatever the reason, I know that saying, "I love you" not only lets the other person know how I feel, but it also fills my heart with joy. And I take comfort in knowing that if something were to happen to me today, the once I love would know how I feel. They would never question our relationship.

The reverse is also true. I never want to lose someone and be weighed down with thoughts of, "If only I had told them sooner" or "I wonder if he knew I loved him." That is not a burden I want to carry.

Choose a Better Life by not waiting for a special event or day to celebrate great friendships and family relationships. Give the gift of love. Tell someone you love them today.

Health

Introduction

Good health is a subject that is near and dear to my heart. I came to the realization that my poor health and accompanying high weight, were holding me back from what God wanted for my life – they was interfering with my ability to Choose a Better Life.

So, I embarked on a journey that forever changed me. I admitted my food addiction, found an accountability partner, researched a program that addressed my needs and began loving myself by making wise choices. Along the way I not only shed pounds and got healthy, but I dealt with much of the emotional baggage that was weighing me down, literally.

The old adage "garbage in, garbage out" most definitely applies to our bodies. If we fuel our body's tank with garbage our output (effectiveness, efficiency, quality of life, etc.) is weakened and less than optimal.

The fuel we give our bodies takes many forms, the obvious: food and drink, and the not so obvious: mental stimulation, relationships and emotional support. And just as we have the choice at the gas station as to which level of octane we put in our cars, we have the choice in life as to the quality of fuel we put into our bodies.

It is up to us to take control of our health. We must choose to provide ourselves with the best fuel possible in order to live the best life possible.

-42-

The Bondage of Addiction

I spoke with a friend, I'll call her Susie, who is considering starting the same health/diet plan that changed my life. I am happy for her not because I think she needs to lose weight, but because I know she will benefit from increased health.

The problem Susie is having is one that plagued me for years and kept me from taking control of my life. She loves her addiction, in this case food, more than she dislikes her current station in life. She is having a hard time letting go of her emotional connection to food and even wonders if it's possible.

It is possible.

However, as with any addiction be it drugs, alcohol, sex, television, anything, Susie has to decide that living the way she is is not working for her. This is the same realization I had to come to. I finally hit the point where I understood that if I kept feeding my addiction I would never obtain the life I wanted and I would never be free of the bondage of poor health.

I had to realize that my life was just not working for me. I was missing out on too much living and letting opportunities pass me by.

I have worked with, and lived with, people who are in bondage to various addictions and regardless of the vice, everyone is the same. As long as they are feeding their addiction they are, in essence, accepting life the way it is. They are willing to trade a healthy, vibrant life for the substance to which they are addicted.

Sound harsh? Maybe. But it's true. There are numerous programs that offer help to anyone who is truly seeking. Help for every addiction. The addict just has to be willing to ask.

That being said, we need to be honest about our addictions, we all have them, and the impact they are having on our lives. If we are unwilling to give up the addiction we need to admit it. We owe ourselves and those who love us at least that much. But if we are tired of living in bondage, we need to seek help.

On the other side of things, we also need to be willing to help those who are seeking our assistance. Letting go of addictions is not easy and we should be supportive by offering grace and accountability when possible.

For Susie, I can only offer a listening ear and advice when asked. I cannot make the decision for her. She must be committed to letting go of her addiction and to reclaiming her life for herself. It is possible, but SHE must decide she is worthy of Choosing a Better Life.

Choose a Better Life by deciding you are worthy of the healthy lifestyle you desire. Be honest about any addictions you may have and choose to enlist support in releasing them.

- 43 -

Plan to Be Healthy

We make daily choices that affect our health. Do I eat that cookie or do I focus on my salad? Do I get a quick snack at the coffee shop or do I wait until I get home to eat some veggies? Do I get up early to exercise or do I sleep the additional 30 minutes?

That being said, many people want a guarantee that they'll make wise choices. Unfortunately, there is no guarantee for good decision making. However, there are steps we can take to increase the likelihood we will make better choices.

Determine the end goal. Why are you taking steps to get healthy? Is it because you have a current health condition you want to improve? Are you looking to increase your energy level? Sleep better at night? Lower your blood pressure? Lose weight? Look better and feel better? Whatever your reason, make sure you know why you are pursuing good health and keep it before you.

Set realistic goals. Nothing is more discouraging that getting to the end of the month only to discover you have lost only 5 of the 20 pounds you were shooting for. However, the opposite is also true; you will be more motivated to continue your health pursuits when you reach mini goals. Nothing says "keep going" more than success.

A healthy weight loss goal is 2-3 pounds a week. More than that and you may be putting more stress on your body than you are doing it good. But perhaps your health goals are to decrease your blood pressure and get off medication. You would be setting yourself up for defeat if you expected to reach that goal in just a few weeks. Talk with your doctor about a healthy, steady decrease in your numbers. For someone who has not exercised, maybe a doable goal is to walk three times a week. It's definitely not to run a 10K marathon at the end of the first month.

Enlist others. The road to good health is a journey that is traveled best with a friend or two. Are there friends or co-workers who would be willing to walk with you several days a week? Do you have someone you can ask to be your accountability partner? Will she be willing to ask you the tough questions? Will you be willing to answer? Find others who are of like mind and join forces with them. You will inspire each other along the way.

Plan. Take time to plan your week. When will you exercise? Can you realistically fit an hour at the gym into your lunch break? Do you need to pack your gym bag the night before and leave it by the front door so you won't forget it? What will you eat for meals and snacks during the week? Do you need to prepare several meals over the weekend and freeze them? Do you need to stock your desk with healthy munchies so you won't run to the snack machine? You will be a lot less likely to be caught off guard if you have planned your week.

Experiment. If you have not exercised in a long time, be willing to try different things. Most gyms offer free week passes without your having to join. Try one to see if you like the gym scene. Do you prefer using an exercise tape in the privacy of your own home? If so, go to a used bookstore and pick up a few different ones. See which you like best. How about walking? When is the last time you walked? Do you enjoy walking more in the morning or evening?

Experiment with foods too. If you can no longer use salt, try different spices. Go to a farmer's market and talk to growers about the different herbs and how they are used. Compare the difference of using fresh herbs to dried ones. Use a food dehydrator to dry several types of fruits and veggies to see which you like best. Have a potluck with your health partners and ask everyone to bring a different dish. You may be surprised just how many different foods you enjoy.

Take action. This is the most important step. You can set goals and plan all you want, but if you don't take action nothing will change. You've heard the definition of insanity –

doing the same thing over and over and expecting different results. The same is true of your health. If you don't take action you are actually choosing to remain exactly where you are now.

Choose a Better Life by choosing to take time to develop a plan for good health that works for you. Then stick to it.

Exercise Your Attitude

My accountability partner and I talk frequently, sometimes daily, committing our plan of action for good health to one another. During a recent conversation we were discussing exercise and our willingness to be willing to do it.

At this particular time she had been struggling with even having the desire to get out and walk. But she shared about her previous day saying that she decided to walk regardless of how she was feeling.

So, walk she did – for a mile. That was first thing Friday morning. At the end of her walk she had a renewed outlook on her day and a great deal of energy. By noon she had accomplished everything she had planned for the day. This left her with some additional time to take care of tasks that had become "B priorities". She went on to say she felt so good all day that she walked a second time that evening.

And on the morning of our conversation, Monday morning when we are so often dragging ourselves into the work week, my accountability partner got up a few minutes early and walked again. Her brisk walk gave her the energy she was hoping for and as she drove to work (that's when we chat each morning) she was looking forward to a good day.

Amazing what a short walk around the block can do for our attitudes. My partner choose to have a better life and a better day just by making the decision to walk before work.

What is your choice? If you can't fit in a walk before work, how about on your lunch break? How about on a 15 minute mid-morning or afternoon break? Can you find time after dinner? If you have a family, take them with you. Have a dog? He'd love to go. Afraid to go out on your own? Grab a friend. Don't want to walk in your neighborhood? Go to a park. Weather not right? Walk in the mall.

We can come up with a long list of excuses why exercise just doesn't fit into our schedule. But excuses they are. Very few of us have real obstacles that keep us from enjoying some type of exercise.

Choose a Better Life by committing to doing something good for yourself today. Commit to finding the time, somewhere in your schedule, to get your body moving. Not only is it good for your health, but it is also good for your attitude.

-45-

De-Stress

According to a September 2007 study by the American Psychological Association 79% of people say stress is a fact of life. In September 2008 the APA released a study saying that stress among women is even higher – 84% depending on the topic. And from my conversation with people around the world, it is safe to say that stress is not just an American issue. People are stressed.

That being the case, we can all benefit from some basic information on dealing with, and reducing, stress in our lives. Here are seven of my favorite tips:

Prioritize. If you are running from task to task and feeling drained at the end of the day, maybe you are trying to accomplish too many things at once. Set priorities. What is it that really needs to be completed today? What do you need to do yourself and what can you delegate to others? What tasks can wait until tomorrow, or even later, to be finished? Will your home life <u>really</u> fall apart if all the chores are not done today?

Be activity efficient. Group similar activities together to accomplish more in less time. For example, pay all of your bills at once. That way you only need to access your banking material at one time. Do the same with running errands, returning calls, completing paperwork, filing forms, etc.

Eliminate invaluable distractions. If you find yourself being easily distracted ask yourself if you really want to take the detour. If the answer is yes, enjoy the distraction, but if no, get back on task. Also, remove distraction temptations from your sight. For example, if email is a problem, inactivate the email received prompts on your computer.

Organize your home and office. Get rid of extra clutter in your space. Clutter not only takes up space, but it also takes time to maintain – dust, organize, rearrange, sort, etc. Clutter also makes it difficult to relax and focus.

Say, "No." It is okay to say, "No" to activities and responsibilities. In fact, it is healthy to do so. You need to know your boundaries and defend them. There will always be people asking for your time and commitments, but it is up to you to know your priorities and care for them. There is no shame in not taking on additional activities that encroach on your precious time.

Say, "Yes!" to you time. Make time for yourself on a weekly, quarterly and yearly basis. Weekly, take advantage of a cancelled meeting by taking a walk or doing something fun. Even better, schedule a meeting with yourself. Put it on your calendar and defend that time. Quarterly, plan an overnight getaway just for yourself. A night of fun without work or responsibilities. Yearly, take time to have a personal retreat; several days to get away to clear your mind, rest and restore your spirit.

Maintain a positive attitude. I can't emphasize this enough. Of all the tips this is the most important. We cannot always choose our circumstances, but we can always choose our attitudes. Choose to focus on the blessings, the good things (a friendship, a roof over your head, the sunlight streaming through the window, even a flower in a jelly jar) and enjoy them with gratitude.

Choose a Better Life by choosing to reduce stress. With each ounce of stress you release you will become a better parent, spouse, boss, employee and friend.

-46-

Kitchen Sabotage

We all know that obesity leads to poor health and increases the stress on our bodies making us more likely to fall prey to things like heart attacks. I've also read statistics that directly link obesity to increased health care costs; makes sense. So, it seems safe to say that being obese costs more than your health, it also costs you dollars. Finances alone are a great motivator to sliming down to a healthy weight.

There are many tips on steps we can take in addition to exercise that would help our weight loss efforts. Over the past year or so I've taught myself to implement many of these ideas just by being aware of my food triggers.

For instance, when my daughter bakes cookies she knows she must package and freeze them as soon as they are cooled. By doing so the cookies are out of sight and not a temptation for me, but easily accessible by her. In fact, this method works perfectly because she can put a frozen cookie in her lunch in the morning and by the time she is ready to eat it it has thawed, but not melted.

Something else we've learned (it's sad that my daughter had to learn this, but having a food addict as a mom brings tough lessons) is that when she bakes something that doesn't freeze well, muffins for example, she packages them in individual servings and hides them in the back of the pantry without telling me where they are. Again, out of sight, out of mind for me, but ready to go for her.

Another "trick" I've learned is to NEVER buy food-scented candles, the ones that are pumpkin pie or sugar cookie fragrances, for example. The only thing those do is stir my cravings, bring images of desserts to my mind and make me falsely hungry – all things I try to avoid. A funny anecdote- the home scents tactic was one our realtor taught us when we were selling our home several years ago. Whenever we had an open house planned we baked cookies or a pie just before the open house was to begin. The scent of dessert was supposed to make people feel relaxed and "at home". If there wasn't time to bake, I'd light one of those food-scented candles for the same reason. Now I only light aromatherapy candles.

Choose a Better Life by becoming conscientious of your surroundings Take a few minutes and stroll through your kitchen. Are there temptations causing you to stumble? Do you have food traps that are just waiting to sabotage your good health? If so, take a few minutes to rearrange things. It will be a small investment of time with a large, long-term payoff.

- 47 -

Patient, Care for Yourself

As patients we have a responsibility to know about, and take charge of, our health care. I am not advocating complete self-diagnosis nor am I suggesting that traditional medicine does not have its place. Doctors, hospitals and prescriptions can definitely be of value. However, as is all too often the case, we tend to run to the doctor for the most minor of illnesses and injuries.

These well-meaning doctors, succumbing to pressure from pharmaceutical companies and our desire to be "cured," are quick to prescribe pills. In our ignorance we accept prescriptions for medications without knowing exactly what we are taking and/or the potential side effects.

As a former pharmacy tech, many of my customers were clueless about the prescriptions I was selling them. And more times than I'd like to acknowledge, customers didn't even know which symptom(s) the medicine was supposed to address. They just blindly accepted the pills and paid the bill.

For years I was no different. I didn't understand that I had not only the right, but the responsibility, to ask questions of my doctors. In an ideal world my doctor would be looking out for only my best interest and would discuss my options before prescribing medications.

However, the reality of current trends in medicine is that most doctors are overworked, burdened with caseloads they cannot possibly serve, working with less and less resources and more and more requirements from the healthcare industry, and are constantly bombarded by pharmaceutical companies. The field of medicine is not what it used to be.

Again, I am not blaming doctors. I believe most of them went into their chosen profession with good hearts and plans to help people live a healthier life. But things have changed over the past several years and doctors can no longer dedicate the amount of time and wisdom it takes to treat individual patients with the same care that was standard many years ago.

That being the case, it is our responsibility to listen to our bodies, become knowledgeable about our medications and understand our alternatives. Not every cold or cough requires antibiotics, for example. In fact, antibiotics can become harmful to our bodies if we take them needlessly.

We must, as much as is possible, become aware of what our illnesses are telling us. Are we feeling nauseous and dizzy because we are sick or are we just dehydrated? Is my heartburn due to acid reflux or am I simply eating foods to which I am allergic? Are my joints achy and stiff because I have arthritis or am I just overweight and out of shape? Are my flu-like symptoms caused by a bacteria or a virus?

If indeed drugs are necessary, we need to ask questions. Is there a different (and cheaper) drug that will target just my illness as opposed to broad-spectrum drugs that fight everything? What are the potential side effects? Will this new medicine interact with any other prescriptions I may be taking?

Also, this is research you will probably need to do on your own, are there alternatives to medications? Are there supplements that have been proven to help my condition? Am I eating something that is causing my problems? Are there food allergies that are triggering symptoms?

Personally I fall into this latter category. A few years ago I was on seven different medications, many to counteract the side effects of other medications I was taking. I took these medications for many months and did not see any relief from my symptoms. In fact, I was getting worse. Thankfully, through a string of events I had to stop taking my prescriptions. After I stopped my health stayed the same, I did not get well, but I did not get worse either.

Then, as I took steps to become aware of what my body was saying to me I realized I had vitamin and mineral deficiencies as well as food allergies. As I changed my eating and began supplementing my diet my symptoms began disappearing. I was able to increase my physical activity and maintain a "normal" lifestyle.

I am, however, very aware that as soon as I fall back into old eating habits my symptoms return. I become tired, my mind sluggish, my joints achy and stiff, I begin having headaches, I get Irritable Bowel Syndrome symptoms and the list goes on. These are the same symptoms that lead to an initial diagnosis of Fibromyalgia several years ago.

If I was not aware of my body's needs I would run straight to the doctor with these symptoms and be put again, on a host of needless medications. Instead, by getting my eating back on track, taking my supplements and increasing my activity my symptoms disappear and I am again healthy.

Choose a Better Life by knowing your body and what it is telling you. Ask questions of doctors, research possible alternatives and then make the decision that is best for you.

- 48 -

Want It or Afraid of It?

I attended a conference where one of the keynote speakers quoted Bill Cosby. Cosby said,

"Decide that you want it more than you are afraid of it."

I love this quote because it pertains to most areas of life. I believe many of us do not pursue our goals because we are either afraid of failure or because we are afraid of success. We become comfortable in our current circumstances even if those circumstances are causing misery.

My health is a great example. For years I was overweight, horribly fatigued, sick and limited in my ability to live. I spent many of those years thinking about getting well, researching steps to do so, and starting and stopping multiple programs. When I was finally honest with myself I realized that I had been hiding behind my poor health – using it as an excuse for my limitations and failures.

In my mind, my business was not successful because my declining health limited the amount of time I could devote to becoming successful. I also on some level believed people were not hiring me because I was obese. So I used these excuses to justify my poor business performance. Subconsciously I knew that if I eliminated these obstacles and became healthy I would no longer be able to hide behind them. I was afraid I would still be unsuccessful and then everyone would know I had been living a lie.

Now I did not purposely become sick and overweight. I initially had little control over my circumstances. However, I allowed my circumstances to become excuses and I choose to wallow in those excuses instead of fighting my disease. My fear of getting healthy outweighed my desire for it. And as a result I wasted many years of my life. Years I am never able to get back.

We are not always deliberate in our sabotage, but I do believe we allow our fears to manifest themselves in ways that limit our success. (Success is not only defined by career or status, it is defined in many other ways including: our faithfulness to our calling, our nurturing a happy marriage, our willingness to take risks, our follow-through on commitments, etc.) So often we settle for much less than life has to offer.

Choose a Better Life by deciding you want it (whatever "it" is) more than you are afraid of it. Then, stop making excuses. Bind your fear and go for it.

- *49* -

Financial Health

I grew up in a home where I was told, "There are three things you never talk about: finances, politics, and religion." And as a family, we never discussed those things.

I, on the other hand, believe there is nothing we should not talk about with family, friends, co-workers or anyone else for that matter. And many of my best discussions have been with people who don't agree with my point of view. That's okay. I welcome the opportunity to hear someone's heart.

One topic, though, seems to have more commonalities than differences is personal finances. I've had many conversations with people who are struggling financially ... people who come up short at the end of the month ... people who are looking for some way to relieve the pressure of finances.

I am definitely not an expert in this field, but I believe people are so open with me because I have always been open about my finances. In 2001 my husband and I lost our consulting firm in a joint business venture that went bad. As a result we went through all of our savings; our investments; lost our health insurance and life insurance, and eventually lost our home.   And with the events of 9/11 we found ourselves without full time employment for the next three years.

It was an incredibly challenging time in our lives, but it was also a time of amazingly rich blessings and we both say we'd not trade that experience for anything. We learned many things about ourselves, our family, our friends, our marriage and our faith. But one of the greatest lessons was in the area of our finances.

When we could not pay our bills it was abundantly clear that we had been living way beyond our means. Prior to our financial crisis, if we saw something we wanted, but didn't have the cash to pay for it, we put it on credit. Our justification was that we would make the money in the next business transaction so there was no need to worry. The problem was we had no guarantees of future earnings so were sacrificing our future for our immediate gratification.

One of the steps we took in getting our financial feet back under us was to adjust our expectations. Just because we saw something we wanted, didn't mean we needed to buy it. Desire does not equal need. We then stopped spending on credit. If we didn't have the cash available to spend, we didn't buy it. Period. We then evaluated every area of our lives and took an honest look at where we could cut back or downsize, again, adjusting our expectations.

The years that followed were not easy. It's never fun to tell your kids, "No, we can't buy the shoes you want. We have to look for something else, something less expensive." Or

"Honey I'm sorry, but we can't go out for your birthday this year. We have to have a party at home." And then there were the difficult days of trying to stretch our food stamps so they would cover a month's worth of groceries. No, it was not easy. But the experience taught us so much and we will forever be grateful.

The live-within-your-means lesson is one we integrated into our lifestyle and still follow today. We do not have credit cards and have no intention of getting any. We have a monthly budget and only increase our spending when our income increases. Within our budget we have included a cushion for unexpected expenses. If we don't need that cushion one month we carry it over to the next. We have worked diligently in paying down our debt and aside from our house and cars we are virtually debt free. And to help alleviate the feeling of being controlled by our money we each get a small monthly allowance that we can spend any way we want. No strings attached.

This is a similar method to the one I used as a teenager. I started working when I was 14 and covered many of my own expenses. To keep track I literally had one envelope for each of my expenses. I would then cash my check and divide it into the appropriate envelopes. If there was no money in the envelope to spend I either had to take money from another or go without.

One of the most freeing things about budgeting is that you control your money. It does not control you. You decide how and when to spend it and whether or not an item is worth the sacrifice of another. And as an added benefit, you have the joy of knowing that you are building your future on a solid foundation rather than compromising it for today's gratification.

Choose a Better Life by choosing to take control of your money. Design a budget that works for you. Live within your means. Pay down debt. Begin to save and invest. Then rest assured you are making the best decisions possible.

- 50 -

Say "No" to the Good

I went to a business networking event. There were about 100 business people from our area talking, making connections and sharing great ideas. What I found interesting, however, is that two of my more prominent conversations had nothing to do with business, per se. Instead, we discussed the need to "take care of ourselves."

By taking care of ourselves I don't mean we need to "watch our backs," "look out for number one" or do "whatever it takes to climb the corporate ladder." On the contrary, we need to simply take time to care for our own emotional, spiritual and physical needs. As one gentleman put it, "Everyone talks about it, but no one does it."

You need to do it. You need to give yourself time to nurture your spirit; time to decompress, relax, reflect and rejuvenate.

How you do this is up to you. You may find that a long bubble bath does the trick. Or maybe it's a walk in the park, or a trip to the beach or the mountains. It could be as simple as going to the library, checking out and reading a good book.

Maybe building something with your hands is what relaxes you or sitting in a café journaling. Whatever it is, it is important to make time for you; your needs are important.

Without the time to decompress we run from task to task stressed out which eventually leads to burn out. And when we are stressed and/or burned out we are of no value to those around us.

You've come across people like this. They are tired, snippy, grumpy and much less effective in everything they do. These are the people who look to be holding it together, but in spending just a few minutes with then you realize they are on the verge of snapping. They are either frantically living or walking around in a semi-comatose state just trying to cope.

All too often we allow ourselves to get to this point because we won't stop and take time for ourselves. We make the excuse that time for ourselves is selfish, but the reality is that time for ourselves is necessary for us to serve those around us – both in our personal and professional lives.

"But I don't have the time to take a walk, or read a book, or pamper myself." The truth of the matter is that we can always make time for our priorities even if that means saying "No" to commitments and opportunities.

In fact, saying "No" is one of our best weapons against burn out. We are inundated with good opportunities. Opportunities to join teams and committees, to mentor people coming behind us, to give our time pro bono, to take on another project, to serve in civic groups, the list goes on. I am a great proponent of these things and participate in many of them myself.

However, I've learned that I cannot accept every opportunity that comes my way. I must say "No" to good things in order to maintain my sanity. I must leave time in my schedule to take care of myself or I will not do anything well. As a result I often say "No" to the good in order to accept the great.

Choose a Better Life by choosing to care for your own needs. As you do you will be better equipped to serve those around you and you will excel in your commitments.

God-Sightings

- 51 -

Introduction

God happens. He is constantly at work around us, but we so often overlook Him. Do we see the ways he cares for, and protects, us? Do we acknowledge Him when we enjoy the beauty of our environment?

Do we see His creativity and gentleness in the way a momma bird feeds her babies?

How about His power – do we sense His power working through us when we speak to an audience? When we stand for truth and justice?

Do we sense His compassion when we read about the baby hippo that was adopted by a 130-year old tortoise (www.owenandmzee.com)?

God is at work around us – all the time. But so often we overlook the Holy because we are distracted; distracted by the mundane and the busyness of life.

May our eyes be opened to the miracle of God's hand at work around and through us. Let's choose to see Him. Choose a Better Life by having eyes for God-sightings.

- 52 -

Friendship Thrives in Freedom

"There can be no friendship where there is no freedom. Friendship loves a free air, and will not be fenced up in straight and narrow enclosures."

William Penn

I have been blessed with several dear friends throughout my life. At this very moment I can pick up the phone and call on any one of several women knowing they will laugh with me, cry with me, pray for me or support me in whatever way I need. I know this is not the case with everyone and I don't take my dear girlfriends for granted. I treasure them and pray for them often.

In fact, as soon as I knew I was moving to Raleigh, NC I began praying for kindred spirits, special girlfriends. I didn't know anyone in Raleigh, but I knew I needed a friend, or two, with whom I could be completely open and honest. I needed a friend who would love me for me and not judge my actions or decisions. I also needed that friend to love me enough to be willing to hold me accountable and "call me on the carpet" when I need it.

My treasured girlfriends are ones who give me the freedom to be myself, good qualities and bad. They listen to my heart's cries and don't try to change them or "fix" them. They don't tell me I'm wrong for feeling a certain way because they understand feelings are neither right or wrong, they are feelings. When the time is right, they do, however, help me to see that sometimes my perceptions are wrong and those wrong perceptions may lead to unnecessary pain or wrong thinking.

But mostly, my kindred spirits just love me and allow me to love them in return. This is the freedom William Penn talks about in his quote. And friendship thrives in freedom.

Are you giving your friends the freedom to be their authentic selves? Do you feel the freedom to drop your walls and take off your masks with others? Most of us have been hurt along the way so authenticity can be frightening at first. If that is true of you, pick one person with whom you feel safe and share your heart. You may be surprised by her response.

A few days ago a girlfriend said to me, "Stephanie, because you were so open with me the first time we met, I knew it was okay for me to be open with you too." This friendship has blossomed since then and I truly count this woman among the great blessings in my life.

Choose a Better Life by choosing to be authentic with others understanding that authenticity doesn't require you to divulge your deepest pains or darkest secrets with everyone you meet. But by removing your masks and being "real" you will know when you are in the presence of a kindred spirit.

- 53 -

The Intimacy of God

I know I shouldn't be, but I am always amazed when God does something so personal there are no words to describe it. This happened for a special friend of mine and I was blessed to be a part of it.

My friend and I meet once a week for brunch. It is a great time of sharing and encouragement. Although I was planning to see her again before Christmas I felt moved to give her her gift early. The gift itself was not a big deal, just a simple ornament that my daughter and I had made placed in a simple gift box.

The night before, I was contemplating exactly which ornament to give ... the pink and white one or the purple and white one. Even though I was leaning towards giving the purple ornament I choose the pink one. I carefully placed it in the gift box and set it on the counter for my morning delivery.

But before I was able to deliver the gift, my daughter opened the box to see which ornament I had chosen. As she did, the ornament fell and shattered on the floor. Although I was disappointed, I knew I had the purple ornament left. So, after cleaning up the broken glass, I carefully placed the purple gift in the box.

When my friend opened the box at brunch she began to cry. I had no way of knowing, but her Christmas tree was decorated with only purple and white ornaments. As she carefully admired the ornament I had just given her, she explained the significance of those two colors in her life.

After years of pain and anguish, God began healing her heart. In May of 2007 she took a personal retreat. During her time away God began pouring his salve of grace on her wounds and enabled her to forgive those who caused her so much pain. Just before she left her retreat God gave her a special message just for her. As part of that message He told her that purple and white represented who she was to Him. White because she is pure before Him and purple because she is part of His royal family.

I had known my friend took this retreat, but I didn't know about her special message, and I didn't need to. Because God knows each of us intimately, better than we even know ourselves, he knew what my friend needed that particular morning. He knew that because of a difficult time the previous night she needed to be reminded of who she was in Him. And He used the brokenness of a pink ornament to bring wholeness and encouragement through a purple one.

I am honored that I was able to be a vessel for God's message to my friend. And I am truly amazed by the ways he meets our heart's deepest needs. The intimacy found in a relationship with the Creator of the universe can be compared to nothing else.

Choose a Better Life by choosing to allow God to meet your deepest needs and experience the abundant joy that can only be found in a relationship with him.

- 54 -

Power and Creativity

I have been blessed with many wonderful experiences (dancing in the Super Bowl, swimming with dolphin in Tahiti, spending the summer in the former Yugoslavia and others) and I am anticipating many more. During my recent trip back to California I was given another one of these extraordinary experiences.

One of my favorite activities in California is dolphin and whale watching with the crew of Captain Dave's Dolphin Safari. I have been dolphin watching on both the Atlantic and Pacific oceans and Captain Dave's Safari is by far the best experience. My recent expedition marks my third safari with Captain Dave's.

On this June day I took my mom (her first trip with Captain Dave's) and my daughter (her second) to Dana Point to board a catamaran for a two-hour safari. As an ocean nut, there is almost no place I'd rather be than on the water. So, any day on the ocean is a good day. But on this particular Tuesday we were especially blessed.

Earlier in the day the crew had seen two blue whales and they were hoping to find one of them again. We traveled several miles out and to our delight the captain spotted one of the whales in the distance. With my daughter and me standing on the front point of the catamaran we headed towards this amazing animal.

With patience and the captain's knowledge it wasn't long before we were just a few hundred feet from the blue whale. I was in awe. This whale, the largest animal on earth, was moving through the water just a stone's throw away from us. She was estimated to be 75 feet long with a tail that was as wide as our boat. Just three feet of her weighed more than our entire catamaran. Her heart alone was the size of a small car. She was amazing to watch.

As we stood on the arm of the catamaran closer to this giant animal than most people will ever be, I realized that with just one swipe of her tail she could break the boat to pieces. It would take but an ounce of her strength to turn us into matchsticks. The power contained in this animal is more than I can imagine. And here we were sailing next to her and often above her as she dove. Amazing!

A few times while the whale was diving the captain turned the catamaran towards a pod of Risso's dolphins. Although I have seen other large pods of dolphin while with Captain Dave's, this day was even more special. Risso's are shy and not as common as other dolphin making them harder to spot. However, here we were enjoying about 100 of them.

If you've seen dolphin in the wild there is nothing like it. They are playful, talkative and incredibly graceful. As they glided through the water we could hear them "speak" to one another. The sound was amazing as the clicks surrounded the catamaran. These wild dolphin would jump in the air as if they were trained. In fact, prior to my safaris with Captain Dave's I thought show dolphin had been trained to do just that, jump and play. Not so. They do it in the wild as part of their natural way of life.

Throughout our expedition, we would alternate between the large, powerful whale and the elegant dolphin. What an amazing experience. There are just no words to describe the overwhelming sense of God: his power and strength of which we got just a glimpse in the blue whale and his creativity and playfulness of which he put but a drop in the beautiful Risso's dolphin.

I am in awe of the Creator who is more than my feeble mind can comprehend. And I am forever thankful for this small glimpse of Him he allowed me to experience.

I am also thankful that we don't need extraordinary experiences to see God. He makes himself known to us each and every day if only we look.

Choose a Better Life by being willing to look and see God all around you.

- 55 -

Intuition

I love the fact that when my heart is right I see God-sightings all around me. Not a day goes by when I don't see God's hand in something that touches my life.

This day was no different.

For several weeks prior I'd had a "service" warning light that occasionally came on when I was driving. When it first happened I had just picked up my car from the shop because of a broken fuel pump. I called the dealer and inquired about the service light and was told not to worry about it because it was probably just resetting from the replaced fuel pump. So, I didn't worry about it.

However, as the weeks went on, the light came on more frequently. Then I noticed that when I would make a right hand turn while braking, my brake light came on as well. "Humph, that's interesting," I thought, "but I'm not gong to worry about it."

It seemed with each passing day both lights came on more than they went off. I began thinking I needed to get my car back to the shop. But several people had advised me that neither light was a big deal and that the car was fine, after all, it drove well. Besides, I didn't have time to take my car to the shop. But my intuition kept nagging me telling me I needed to get the car serviced.

So I made time to take it to the shop first thing the next morning. I had a great chat with one of the men who works there and enjoyed talking with the shuttle driver who brought me home all the while wondering if I was over-reacting to these lights. "Better safe than to be sorry," I reasoned.

A short while later I received a call saying that indeed there was a problem with the car. The brakes were about to go out and needed replacing. A few hours later the shuttle driver was back in my driveway and off we went to the dealership where I have my car serviced.

After I picked up my car I was driving my daughter on an errand for an upcoming trip and I was overwhelmed with gratitude. "Thanks God for keeping me safe despite my failing brakes and for prompting me to take the car into the shop."

Had I not listened to my intuition who knows what awful thing may have been awaiting me. At the very least, I could have been greatly inconvenienced had my brakes failed on the way to a client workshop or the next week on the way to my personal retreat 200 miles away from home. However, since the car was fixed I was able to drive with confidence knowing it was safe.

Choose a Better Life by choosing to listen to your intuition. It may just be God's still small voice protecting you from a disaster.

- 56 -

Road Trip

During the summer of 2008, I spent 12 days on a 1600 mile road trip with my mom and youngest daughter. We visited the gorgeous mountains of western North Carolina, drove through the rolling hills of Tennessee, enjoyed both sides of the great state of Virginia, visited the harbor in Baltimore and ended up on the beach in Virginia Beach.

Throughout the trip we stopped and visited with friends and family … some I had not seen since I was a child – over 30 years ago. What a joy it was to spend time with them again.

One thought repeatedly ran through my mind while I was on this trip, "Wow, this is amazing!" Whether I was standing at the top of a 2280 foot mountain in the Blue Ridge Parkway, at the bottom of a 404 foot waterfall, or sitting on the beach looking out into the Atlantic Ocean I was mesmerized by the beauty of creation. And even though my eyes saw my surroundings I could not fully comprehend the beauty. The more I tired to take it in, the more I realized I just couldn't digest it all. Thinking of just one color ... there are hundreds, if not thousands, of shades and hues of green.

The night before we left for home, I was sitting on the beach watching both kids and adults play in the ocean as the waves rolled onto shore. In the distance I could see a few boats and cruise ships pass by. All the while I was thinking that for as much as I see above the water, there is another world below it as well. A world full of colors and animals I've rarely seen.

As I was trying to wrap my mind around this bounty of life, I realized that I am but a minuscule part of creation. In light of the universe I am but a grain of sand. And the "issues" that I deal with are virtually non-existent by comparison. I realized just how small I really am.

And yet, as tiny as I seem, I know that nothing matters more to the Creator of this amazing universe than I do. I am not dwarfed by creation in the eyes of God. He sees me, He knows me (warts and all), He loves me, and He is overjoyed by the thought of me. And with everything that happens each second of each day, God is not distracted from me.

The same is true of you. Despite the enormity of creation, God knows the number of hairs on your head. He knows every thought that passes through your mind and every emotion you feel. And amazingly, his love for you never waivers. He loves you with a love that is deeper than the oceans and higher than the tallest mountain.

Choose a Better Life by choosing to embrace your standing in this universe and in the eyes of the Creator. Nothing is more important to God than you.

Harley: A True Love

God-sightings can occur anywhere. Since He is the Creator his fingerprints are around us everywhere we look.

One of the places I see Him most often … in Harley, my Husky/Australian Shepherd Mix.

Having come from the pound, Harley is grateful just to have a home. She never complains, even when she is sick, and she is always thankful. After almost every meal she will come over, lick her chops and wag her tail. I know it is her way of saying, "Thank you for dinner."

Her companionship is amazing. Since I work from home I get to spend many hours with her. Even if she doesn't want to be petted, she is always by my side. If I walk from my upstairs office to the downstairs to pick something up, she comes with me. When I go back to the office she lays down so she can see me at all times. When I go to the kitchen to fix lunch, yes, she is there.

My husband says she even picks up on my moods. If I'm sick or not feeling well she is quiet and acts as a caretaker. If I am upset she is docile and demure. If I am watching TV and yelling at a hockey game, she is in the other room or upstairs (she does not like loud voices). My husband even jokes that when he comes home from work he can tell if I'm in a good mood or not just by the way the dog responds when he comes in.

Her behavior that I love the most? Welcome home greetings. As soon as she hears my car pull up in the driveway she goes to the front window to watch me walk up to the house. I can see her from the driveway and immediately it puts a smile on my face. By the time I reach the front door I can hear her on the other side. As I walk in she wiggles and wags as if I've been gone for days. At the same time she kisses any part of skin she can find, legs, hands, arms, my chin... And I swear I can see a smile on her face.

And it is in Harley's unconditional love for me that I get a glimpse of God. For I know that the love I receive from my pup is nothing compared to the love from my Father.

Choose a Better Life by embracing love from the many sources around you.

- 58 -

A Special Gift

Every other month my husband and I host a networking event for contacts in our local area. Typically we have 250-300 people attend, but because of the economy we had just under 350 attendees at this particular event.

Per our usual style, we do not charge for admittance and we do not hold an agenda. We do have 3-4 corporate sponsors who fund the appetizers and several other companies who donate door prizes. (Our request on door prizes is that they have a minimum value of $50. All of our donors have been most gracious and generous.)

A few times throughout the evening my husband makes announcements and we draw for door prizes. Other than that, the three hours is dedicated to networking and making connections.

With nearly 350 names in the fish bowl, I was particularly burdened that Tuesday's door prizes go to people who would benefit from them. Almost to the person the door prizes were a great fit.

At the end of the evening one gentleman stopped me and said he had won a $75 gift card to a local restaurant. He then told me his story. Bill said his luck had been bad recently; he had been laid off and was struggling financially. Both his birthday and his wedding anniversary were within the next 10 days and he was dreading both because he could not celebrate. He was a bit overwhelmed by winning the gift card (he said he never wins anything) and said he could now take his wife to dinner for their anniversary. He was most thankful for having come to the event. I told him the gift card was a special God-gift just for him.

Choose a Better Life by choosing to see the God-gifts in your life.

Love Beyond Measure

One Valentine's Day my husband took me to lunch at a nearby country club. We had a great view of the golf course, the food was wonderful and our time will be treasured. Aside from getting away with my husband, one thing that really stood out to me was an older couple sitting a few tables away.

My guess was that this couple was in their 70s. They did not speak English, but that did not keep me from gazing over at them and "eavesdropping."

The love and pride they have for each other obvious. Although I could not understand their words, there was no doubt they were verbally caressing each other. They both smiled as they talked and very rarely dropped eye contact.

I watched as the husband gently reached across the table grabbed his wife's hand and gave her a gently squeeze. They let go only when dessert was brought to the table and placed between them for them to share.

As thoughts of this couple stayed with me for days I couldn't help but think that this is but a glimpse of God's love for us. God invites us to join him at his feast and when we do, his eyes lock on ours as he reaches across the table to hold our hand. Love and pride gush from his eyes as he speaks gently with words that only our hearts understand.

It was a privilege to sit near this couple on Valentine's Day and to bask in the love they have for one another. And I'm incredibly thankful for their reminder that the Creator of the Universe is that in love with me.

Choose a Better Life by opening your heart to the One whose love for you is beyond measure.

- 60 -

Simple Pleasures

One of the great blessings of being forced to slow down is the opportunity to thoroughly enjoy the simple pleasures in life … the sunlight streaming through my living room blinds, aromatherapy fragrances that fill my office, hearing children laugh as they walk to/from the bus. These are all great things that sometimes got overlooked in my busy life.

This past Saturday was a great day. My youngest daughter and I were able to spend many hours running errands and just "hanging out" together. We tried on shoes and clothes, shopped for make-up and hair dye, shared a plate of Chinese food, and hunted for bargains. We had a great day just being together and laughing.

I have always enjoyed time with my girls, but lately I recognize that those times are more than enjoyable, they are precious. So whenever I have the opportunity I try to put aside my "activity" for the day so I can rearrange my priorities and spend time with my family. I am always so blessed when I do.

Lately I have also become very fond of technology, especially email. The fact that a girlfriend on the other side of the country can type an email while I am asleep so that I receive it when I first logon in the morning is wonderful. I have come to love email as much as I love snail mail. A simple pleasure that brings a smile to my face.

Another simple pleasure that has always brought me an enormous amount of joy is playing with my puppies – in truth, they are almost old enough to be considered senior dogs, but they are still puppies in my mind. Few things sound as wonderful as their tails thumping on the floor – a sign of pure happiness from them – or make me smile as much as seeing them sitting in the window when I pull up.

If I am having a particularly difficult day, all I have to do is hug my puppies and everything seems so much better. They love me unconditionally, wait for me to come home and play with every new toy I bring them. Simply being with them brings me great pleasure.

Choose a Better Life by choosing to look for and enjoy the simple pleasures in your life.

Hodgepodge

- 61 -

Introduction

Many of the tidbits of treasures I have gathered are like life itself, they don't fit neatly into a predetermined section or compartment of life. However, each lesson we're given has value and is meant to grow and strengthen us. For this reason, I have included this last hodgepodge section. It's a collection of unrelated tidbits from various sources, all of which have made a profound impact on me and I hope, on you as well.

Enjoying Life: More than Just Looking for the Good

During the summer of 2007 we were blessed with having our middle daughter stay with us. We've missed our older two daughters terribly since we moved to North Carolina and it was wonderful to connect with one of them again.

Sarah is 18. She is beautiful, amazingly gifted in many areas and incredibly intelligent. She is a sophomore at the University of Southern California, having skipped her senior year of high school. She is also a national merit scholar and has been approached to model. She really is an "it" girl.

But what I love most about Sarah is her love for fun ... good, clean, wholesome fun. She loves her friends, loves life and is always making the best of every situation – even in the little things. For example, as a family we played Monopoly two nights in a row. On both nights Sarah was bankrupted first. However, instead of pouting or even making negative comments she'd laugh and say things like, "See, this is why I wanted to play Monopoly. I knew I'd clean you out." (Yes, this is only a game, but for those of us who are very competitive –

like we are – any opportunity to "take out the competition" can take on a life of its own.)

Sarah also looks for ways to create her own fun. While she was here we took some of the usual obligatory pictures. But what we did on her last day is what made the lasting impressions. She and I took my youngest daughter out of school. We loaded our cameras and headed downtown. Our goal was to shoot some "fun" pictures at a retro coffee shop we had been to earlier in the week, but found it closed when we got there.

We decided to make the best of it and found some other fun picture spots: a few local restaurants with outdoor seating, the downtown park with its 12-foot acorn statue, the Capital lawn with its war statues, and anything else along the way including interesting trash cans. But as Sarah does with all her pictures, she didn't just stand and smile. Instead, we struck poses that were out of the ordinary … jumping in the air, hiding behind menus, imitating statues, etc. and we had a blast. Along the way we also made many people shake their heads, smile, and laugh.

At a time in life when most girls are overly concerned with whether or not every hair is in the right place and whether or not they are making the right impression, Sarah throws "tradition" to the wind and enjoys life. She lives with an abandon that is most impressive.

Over the past few years I have learned to enjoy life too. I am, for the most part, a happy joyful person. I look for the good and I expect to see it. I live anticipating the blessings and miracles that come my way. But after spending time with Sarah I realized that there is still a long way to go. She looks at ordinary circumstances and doesn't just enjoy them, she turns them into extraordinary events; something I had yet to do.

My daughter taught me a very valuable lesson that summer. Enjoying life is about more than just looking for the good – it is about *creating* the good in every situation.

Choose a Better Life by actively creating good and fun situations.

- *63* -

Embracing Your Inner Lemon

This is an activity I do in some of my workshops...

As participants walk into the room they notice that each person's space is set up with a number of items. The one that always seems to grab their attention first is the lemon.

I ask each participant to take a few minutes to "get to know their lemon" ... to look their lemon over and become familiar with it. Then I collect the lemons and randomly arrange them on a table in the front of the room. At this point I ask all the participants, usually between 25-40, to come to the front of the room and find their original lemon.

Surprisingly, most people are successful in finding their original lemon.

My point in this simple activity is that at first glance all lemons look alike, but when you take a few minutes to really look at the lemon you see differences and nuances that are unique to the individual lemon. AND in addition to being unique, each lemon can be successful in its "job" ... in my scenario making lemonade.

People are the similar to lemons. (No, we are not sour.) At first glance we look alike, but when you get to know each of us we are unique individuals with our own style and ways of doing things. However, we each have the same potential to be successful in whatever we set our minds to.

One of my favorite quotes is by St. Francis de Sales. He said, "Do not wish to be anything but what you are, and try to be that perfectly." In other words, don't look at someone else and wish you were more like them. You've been given a wonderful set of characteristics and qualities that make you unique.

Choose a Better Life by embracing your individuality and celebrate what makes you uniquely you. Then know that with determination you can achieve whatever you set your mind to.

- 64 -

Turning Pain Into Blessing

Many times I've pondered the question, "If I had unlimited resources, how would I impact the world?" For me, I can think of nothing worse than getting to the end of my life and realizing I had wasted my time here on Earth. With every ounce of my being I desire to be used by God to impact the lives of those around me and around the globe. I want my life to make a difference for others.

I attended an awards banquet for business men and women in our area. These are men and women who are considered "Movers and Shakers" because they are making a difference in our community. While there I met Jeff.

Several years ago Jeff, and about 400 other people, was laid off from his job. At some point in his job search he realized he and several of his co-workers were not going to be able to find employment. So they decided they would open their own business. As the business became profitable they agreed on three objectives.

The first was to ensure that they, and their employees, earned enough money to care for their families. Once that objective was met they moved to their second: providing great healthcare for their team. They contracted with Blue Cross/Blue Shield to provide some of the best medical benefits in the area. Their final objective was to give back to their employees, so ever quarter in which they are profitable (they have been profitable for 29 quarters in a row), they return 25% of company profits to their employees – every employee gets a share.

Jeff's business has been in existence for six years now and he has over 400 employees. He says that for him and his partners, the most important goal is to take care of their employees. After that, the rest is icing on the cake.

During the night's event Jeff shared a few of the company's "success stories." These stories were not about how much money the company makes or about contracts they have secured. The stories were about people whose lives had been changed. One example was a man who was, in essence, on the streets when he was hired. He had no skills, but Jeff's company believed in him and trained him. He has since gotten his life together, been promoted several times, gotten married, bought a house and is pouring his life back into others. That is success. That is impacting the world.

The more people I meet the more I realize that those who are making a difference in the world seem to have come through a place of pain. (In Jeff's story it was through his own unemployment that he decided to provide for others.) They take their pain learn from it, grow because of it, and turn it around into something positive … something that will impact the world.

Choose a Better Life by choosing to use your pain, struggles and experiences to make a difference in the lives of others.

- 65 -

The Stuff of Stuff

Whether we admit it is true of ourselves or not, we all agree that emotional baggage can weigh us down and hinder our movement. But what about physical baggage …the stuff with which we populate our lives? You know what I'm referring to. The furniture, the books, the decorations, the bric-a-brac. The stuff that seems to be so important to us.

We cherish our stuff. We show it off to friends and guests, we build shelves to display it and buy special boxes to store it. Some people even build homes around their stuff.

I'm not saying any of this stuff is bad. In fact, a lot of it is good. It is nice to have furniture on which to share meals or sit and watch TV. Looking at old photo albums and reminiscing with friends is priceless. But much of our stuff is unnecessary, takes precious time to maintain and causes stress.

Take me for example, I love books. I have a ton of them. So many in fact, that my garage has a dozen or so boxes full of them. These are the books for which I no longer have space in my house. I could buy more bookshelves, find a space in my home for them and unpack. But by doing so, my living space would be crowded and I'd feel claustrophobic and become unproductive.

Then there are times like the other morning. I was looking for something specific in the garage, I found myself moving box after box of books from one side of the garage to the other just so I could gain access to the object for which I was hunting. As I turned to re-enter my house, I realized I had built a fortress around myself with boxes of books. I had to move the boxes back to their original side of the garage just so I could access the door!

So, the question I have to ask myself is this "Is it worth my time to keep all these books?" There are moments I'd like to think so. As a writer I'm always reading, learning and referencing other peoples' work. True. But I've already pulled out the most valuable of my books and found places for them in my home. The books in the garage are ones I rarely riffle through. Besides, with the internet, information is just a few keystrokes away.

A few years ago, my husband and I pared down significantly. We decided that we no longer wanted to be held captive to our stuff. We wanted to be able to pack up and move across the country or to the other side of the world if we wanted to without having to worry about what to do with all our stuff. We did move across the country, but in two short years we had again accumulated so much stuff that our 1800 square foot house is not big enough to hold it all. Pathetic!

I have a girlfriend who is, she and her family, preparing to go overseas as missionaries. During their preparations they sold their home, gave many of their "valuables" to relatives who would care for them and sold the majority of their stuff. Each of their kids was allowed to pack one box – one box – with items they wanted to keep. The rest was gone. At first this sounded a little harsh. But because this family has cut ties with the stuff that weighed them down they were able to spend 7 weeks touring the United States. They saw more of our beautiful country in a few months than most people will see in a lifetime. And this is only the beginning. In several months they will leave the US and travel to several places around the world. What a wonderful journey.

Choose a Better Life by letting go of some of the stuff that so easily weighs us down, cause stress and robs us of our time and freedom.

66

A Small, but Heartfelt Gift

My husband Chuck and I meet once a week for lunch. It is our time to debrief and reconnect. His office is about 30 miles from our home and I make it a priority to block out time to go out there each Thursday. In fact, it is such a routine that last week as I walked up to the building and said hi to two of his co-workers one of them responded, "Wow, is it lunch time already?" Yes, the dinner bell had arrived. ☺

We went to one of our favorite restaurants not far from his office. Beside the fact that it has great food, one of the reasons we love this restaurant so much is that the owners and staff are so friendly. They are flexible in how I put my order together, always smile, always say hi and usually hold some sort of short conversation.

On this particular day Chuck and I were eating outside on the patio. One of the owners pulled up after his delivery, introduced us to his daughter, and chatted for a minute. On his way inside he asked if we needed anything. Chuck jokingly said,

"Yeah, if you're handing out some of your cookies." (He has wonderful cookies.) I quickly followed with "No, no cookies." My salmon and salad were just right. I didn't want the temptation of the cookie. Robert, the partner, smiled, "When she's not here I'll give you a cookie."

Chuck and I finished our lunch and continued talking about life. A few minutes later Robert brought out a manila envelope with Chuck's name on it and said, "Ah, remember the information you asked me for last week?" and handed the envelope to him. Chuck began to open it and Robert quickly said, "You may want to wait to open it." Chuck snuck a peek. Inside was a cookie!

Chuck and I laughed and got great enjoyment out of the gift. Not only had Robert given Chuck a cookie, but he did so without tempting me in the process. It was such a simple thing to do, but it was so much appreciated. Chuck and I talked about this act of kindness all the way back to the office.

As I left Chuck's office and passed the restaurant on my way home, I again thought about the cookie and smiled. Giving this gift took Robert only a few minutes, but it brought an amazing amount of joy to Chuck and me. What a great reminder of how we can do little things to bring happiness to someone else.

Choose a Better Life by giving a simple, but heartfelt gift, a small act of kindness to someone else today.

67

An Attitude of Gratitude

"An attitude of gratitude" that phrase has been thrown around a lot over the years.

So, what is an attitude of gratitude? In short, it is a frame of mind, a way of thinking and looking at life and it can be summarized in one word ... thankfulness.

There is a direct correlation between our level of thankfulness and our quality of life. Thankfulness increases our quality of life while negativity decreases it. Think about it, when we are thankful, our overall mood is upbeat, fun, joyful, and well ... thankful. When we are ungrateful and negative we tend to be grumpy, bitter and angry.

There is no doubt in my mind which of these I'd rather be. So, in an effort to cultivate a continual attitude of gratitude I take time to recount my blessings and bless others. I have also been disciplining myself to speak out loud something positive about every challenging situation that comes my way. A perfect example occurred during a holiday weekend.

Saturday afternoon my family and I returned home after having run errands. I walked into the garage looking for a yard rake and heard what sounded like a waterfall. As I looked around I discovered we had a pipe that had broken in the ceiling and pouring out of it was steaming hot water.

My husband began shutting off valves and I got on the phone with our home warranty company. Eventually we had to have the water to our home shut off in order to stop the flow of water into our garage. In the few hours of chaos it took to get the situation under control I noticed several boxes of books, pictures, office paraphernalia and my husband's Monopoly collection were showing signs of water damage.

After several calls to our home warranty company we realized that a plumber was not going to be able to make it to our home until the following day. We had a choice to make, we could be angry and upset about the situation, or we could have an attitude of gratitude and enjoy the rest of our weekend. We opted for the latter.

What did we have to be grateful about regarding a broken water pipe? Plenty... the pipe that broke was in the garage, not the house, many of the water damaged items in the garage were at least somewhat salvageable, we had just renewed our home warranty four days earlier, a friend gave my husband and me a great rate at a hotel for the night, my daughter stayed the night with another friend and had a great time, the pipe was fixed the next day, and the plumber gave us great information on preventative maintenance for the rest of our pipes. All in all it was a good experience – a good experience because we choose to look for the positive things for which we were thankful.

Just a few days before, I was watching a morning talk show. The topic of discussion was this very thing, how can we be thankful and show gratitude for our challenges. One of the experts in the discussion said this, "A great way to express gratitude is to find a need of yours that has been met and meet it in someone else's life." Her examples included a cancer survivor sitting with a cancer patient who is undergoing treatment and a formerly homeless person serving meals at a rescue mission.

Acts of gratitude don't have to be this dramatic. They can be as simple as being thankful for the location of a broken water pipe. It is not how we show gratitude that is as important as the fact that we recognize our blessings and are genuinely grateful for them.

Choose a Better Life by adopting an attitude of gratitude.

68

Unique as a Leaf

One of the things I have enjoyed most about our move from California to North Carolina is the color of Fall. I love looking out my window and seeing the different hues of red, gold, orange and rust. It's is so beautiful.

With my love of Fall comes the relaxing opportunity to collect leaves of many colors. As I walk any number of trails, I stop every few feet to pick up another bunch of these amazing leaves. I've even gotten my daughter involved. As much as she hates to admit it, she enjoys my version of a nature walk.

As I was out gathering leaves most recently, I noticed something interesting … no two leaves are alike. They may come from the same type of tree, or even the same tree, but they are all unique in one way or another.

There are the obvious differences: color and shape, but many are made different by other catalysts. Some have been nibbled on by a variety of bugs. Some have been torn during their journey from branch to ground. Some have been stepped on once they came to their resting place on the floor below.

As I have examined and gathered leaves over the past few years I've found that I really like the leaves that are not "perfect." The ones that are different. The ones that have some character. The ones that look as if they have "lived" a little.

People are like leaves. Simply, by nature, we are all the same; we come from the same place – God created us all – and we all end up in the same place – standing before Him once we die. But along the way we get bumps, bruises, and tears. Some of us even get nibbled on by life experiences. And it's these life experiences that cause us to be different, to be our own person, to develop character.

It is our life experiences that also develop our gifts and provide us the opportunities to grow. Through them we become stronger and more mature. And by doing so, we often have the opportunity to encourage someone else along the way... to provide her with a shoulder to lean on when she needs it most, reassuring her that she is not alone.

Choose a Better Life by never looking at circumstances as a bar of measurement for any one life and never judge a life by its circumstances. Instead, may we embrace life experiences, ours and others', as a means for growth and personal development. And may we be eternally thankful that God connects us through our individual experiences while using our entire life's experiences to make us unique.

69

Adding Value

Whether you are the CEO of a Fortune 500 company, the janitor at the local high school or a stay-at-home Mom, if you have a job (I consider being a stay-at-home mom a job), you have been given the opportunity to work. And I do mean opportunity.

Opportunity is defined by MSN Encarta as "a chance, especially one that offers an advantage." Working definitely offers advantages. Aside from the obvious financial benefit that comes from a job, work offers the opportunity to use, improve and gain valuable skills. It also opens doors for relationships, education, and independence, among other things.

So my question is this … what value are you adding to your work? What are you bringing to your job that no one else offers? Are you coming to work with a good attitude, ready to pitch in where needed? Or are you looking at your job as a necessary evil?

If you are one of the fortunate ones who has a job, whether or not it is ideal, I propose that you are able to make it better just by changing your attitude towards what you do. Not only does a good attitude help in your outlook on completing the basic tasks required, but it also impacts every person with whom you come in contact.

A specific example sticks out in my mind. My daughter and I were at the airport (she was flying as an unaccompanied minor) and after she boarded the plane I watched the ticket agent as he scanned each passenger's boarding pass. At the end of the line was a young couple with an infant. The couple looked a bit frazzled as they were gathering their belongings.

As the ticket agent was handed their passes he exchanged pleasantries with the couple. I could not hear their conversation, but within seconds the couple's eyes lit up as they were thanking the agent profusely. I watched their interaction and realized the agent had upgraded the family to first class, without charge.

Just as the doors to the boarding area were getting ready to close, a businessman came hurriedly up to the agent. He handed in his boarding pass and walked quickly down the ramp. The agent called him back (I stood a bit closer so I could hear the conversation this time.) and asked if he'd prefer not to sit in a middle seat. The agent said he could change the seat assignment so the man would be able to sit in a row by himself. The man was elated.

Neither of these activities caused the ticket agent an extreme amount of additional work, but both blessed others as they were starting their day. Just by being attentive and willing to make changes, the agent added value to his job and to the airline for which he works. I imagine the young family and the businessman alike will consider flying this airline on their next trip. I know I will.

Choose a Better Life by looking for ways you can add value to your work.

70

Not Limited by Age

Without having clearly stated it my daughter Britini wants to use her life to make a difference.

Ever since she was a toddler she has looked out for the underdog, making friends and inviting them to play with her. As she has gotten older she has learned to take a stand and tell others, her friends included, that there is no need to call someone else names or put her down just because they disagree on an issue.

As much as she can at this age, Britini is even learning that sometimes doing the right thing may cause her heartache and cost her a friendship or two. But regardless, she is always on the lookout for ways to help others.

Her school was doing a fundraiser for the local Leukemia foundation. The students were instructed to bring in money from home (theirs or their parents'). There were no knick-knacks, food stuffs or magazines to buy. Just the cash each family was generous enough to donate. My daughter decided that she and her friends would be more effective if they joined forces and rallied their neighbors.

So, on a particular Friday, Britini invited several friends from class over for a sleepover. Shortly after they all arrived and dropped off their bundles of "stuff" the girls grabbed Ziploc bags and a copy of the school flyer and headed out. They walked our entire neighborhood, some 200 homes, going door to door asking for spare change for the fundraiser. Within a few hours they had gathered over $160 – in coins!

Although the weight of those coins almost killed her, Britini was thrilled to carry them up 6 flights of stairs to her homeroom on Monday morning. Without even thinking much, my daughter had found a simple way to make a difference.

Wanting a more tangible way to serve, a few summers ago Britini decided she would join a group of kids from church on a summer mission's trip. This small group of middle and high school students took a week out of their summer plans to work with and serve an impoverished community in the mountains of West Virginia. For one gentleman who couldn't walk and hadn't been out of his house in years these kids literally gave him renewed hope. The students spent days removing shoulder-high weeds and debris from his front and back yard talking to him through the darkened screen door whenever possible.

The man who had become a recluse and a social outcast managed to get dressed and meet the kids on his front porch a few days into their work. He talked with the kids, shared some of his invention ideas and cried in appreciation for what they had done. It was the first act of kindness this man had received in years.

The next summer a larger group of kids from church, our daughter included, flew to the Bahamas to serve in the same way. They did not stay in a resort or enjoy the typical tourist attractions. Instead they worked alongside locals to help finish construction projects, taught young kids how to do arts and crafts during Vacation Bible School and provided support in any way they were asked. Each of the 22 students who went were in grades 7-9 and they all wanted to serve.

These students are an encouragement and a reminder that anyone, regardless of our station in life, can make a difference for another person. We just have to be willing.

Are you willing? You don't have to do something as dramatic as going to another country. You can serve right where you live. Volunteer at the local rescue mission, teach a class to seniors, take food to an animal shelter or read to students at a nearby elementary school. We ALL can make a difference and we ALL can leave this world making it brighter for just one person.

Choose a Better Life by choosing to make an impact today. You may never know how you change someone's life, but your can count on receiving joy just for being willing.

My CABL Story

71

My CABL Story

Growing up I always felt a bit odd, a little different. (People who know me well are still saying I'm a bit odd, but that's okay. I know they mean it in love. ☺) I wasn't content just accepting the status quo.

I enjoyed doing things people told me I couldn't ... I danced in the Super Bowl when I was told I'd never make it past the first round of auditions. I graduated from college with honors when my parents told me college was not an option for me. I had a corner office by my mid-twenties when I was told I'd never be able to support myself. I enjoyed proving people wrong.

What I didn't understand until years later is that I could have done these things not out of rebellion and stubbornness, but out of love and passion. Love for myself and passion for life.

I've learned that we can be thankful for our past experiences, regardless of what they are, because they all come together to make us who we are today. Today, I can love myself despite what has happened to me or what I've done. I can love myself because my Father in Heaven loves me. He is happy with me and is waiting to pour out his goodness to me. I just have to be willing to accept it.

I can hear the comments now, "Well, yeah, if you've had an easy life you can be thankful for your past, but someone like me, never." So, lest you think my life has been smooth sailing, here is a partial list of things I have experienced: verbal abuse, repeated date rape, alcoholism, sexual promiscuity, a suicide attempt, family imprisonment, death threats, threat of physical abuse, financial devastation and bankruptcy, divorce, false accusations, betrayal, single parenting, serious illness, addiction, depression, obesity and more.

I am definitely not sharing these things because I am proud of them. Quite the contrary. I've experienced my share of pain and I've made some very bad choices in my life, but I can honestly say that I am thankful for the person they have made me today. God promises to use ALL things for the good of those who love him. (Romans 8:28) He didn't say some things, or most things. He said ALL things.

So, here I am today saying that despite the pain of my past my heart overflows with joy. Today I pursue peace, forgiveness, wholeness, wellness, passion, energy, vision, power, dedication and life. This does not mean my life is now free from obstacles. I still have challenges to overcome, but I am working on changing my paradigm. Instead of being angry or wallowing in disappointment (I admit, some days it's harder than others) I am choosing to look at these challenges as opportunities to grow. To become a better wife, mom, daughter, sister and friend.

And at the risk of sounding arrogant or phony, I must say, life is fun. It really is. I am enjoying my life each day and I wouldn't trade it for anyone else's.

I feel like I have finally "arrived." No, I have not reached my final career goal nor have I fit into the size 6 jeans I once coveted. I am not driving a new car or living in a large house. I am not famous nor am I earning the amount of money I'd eventually like to earn. But I am having fun living the life I have been given.

Be it in my personal or professional life I look forward to the day, and how I may be used to make a difference, even be it small, in someone's life ... how I may lighten a friend's burden or encourage someone to "pay it forward." My days, as are yours, are filled with opportunities to bless others.

Amazingly, as I do this for others I find that my life gets better and better too. I'm discovering that positive people are attracted to me, my relationships are growing, my home life is more peaceful, my work more enjoyable, my finances more abundant ... the list goes on and on.

This is not to say that life is without its challenges today. Trust me, I have plenty – a 22-year old daughter who refuses to speak to me for reasons I do not understand; a biological family that is far from healthy; a dear friend on the other side of the country who is hurting deeply and whom I cannot help; and physical pain from injuries that never seems to fully disappear.

But when I think of my life, I don't think of those challenges first. What I think of is the joy I have for living and the abundance of blessings I get to experience every day. I love my life. I really do.

It is no small coincidence that as I began to retrain my mind to focus on the positive and as I began to bless others and myself, the negative things in my life seemed to take up less and less space in my consciousness. Now I have to stop and really think if I want to list my challenges – this is not something I do very often. In fact, I spend so much time listing my blessings and the things that are going well that I often don't have time to think of the challenges. Nor do I want to.

No, I am not living in denial. I am well aware of the areas of life that are less than perfect and I work to do what I can to change them. But I no longer allow them to consume me, overwhelm me, or dictate my moods and feelings. I wasted too many years doing just that. Now I celebrate life and enjoy the fun.

I know the power and authority God has given me as His child to bless instead of curse. I understand my position to claim His promises and walk in them.

Today I practice and work to Choose a Better Life.

Contact Stephanie

Stephanie wants to hear from you. Please send her your thoughts and feelings on this book. She also wants to hear your Choose a Better Life stories.

Send your correspondence to Stephanie Hester at CABLBook@gmail.com

Please include contact information in your email.

If you are sharing a personal CABL story please indicate if you would like to give Stephanie permission to post your story on the Choose a Better Life website.

4663535

Made in the USA
Charleston, SC
26 February 2010